Beyond Argument:

A Handbook
for Editorial Writers

Edited by Maura Casey and Michael Zuzel

Inquiries may be directed to:
NCEW
6223 Executive Blvd.
Rockville, MD 20852

Library of Congress Card No: 00-191708

ACKNOWLEDGMENTS

Like all good editorial pages, this book is a conversation—singular voices reflecting multiple, diverse views. The editors shepherded it from conception to fruition, but they were aided and encouraged (and in some cases rescued) by the ideas, enthusiasm and dedication of many colleagues and advisers around the country.

First and greatest thanks go to Susan Albright, who conceived of *Beyond Argument* long before it had a title and contributed to its realization at every step, even writing an entire chapter. Alongside her stand the National Conference of Editorial Writers, the NCEW Foundation and especially the Scripps Howard Foundation, all of which helped to provide the resources necessary for such an ambitious project.

We particularly thank the officers and members of NCEW who stepped forward to assist us along the way: Lynnell Burkett, Colleen Burns, Meg Downey, Fred Fiske, Phineas Fiske, Froma Harrop, Phil Haslanger, Neil Heinen, Barbara Mantz-Drake, Morgan McGinley, Charles Reinken, Sue Ryon, Kay Semion, Chuck Stokes, John Taylor and Jim Boyd.

As always, the assistance of NCEW's support staff at Everett Associates and our public relations team at Armour&Armour was invaluable. We'd also like to thank Tammy-Jo Ferdula and Skip Weisenburger, both of *The Day* of New London, Connecticut, and Barbara Ireland of *The New York Times*.

Last, we thank our respective employers, *The Day*, and *The Columbian* of Vancouver, Washington. Though separated by a continent, the two institutions share a firm belief in opinion pages as vital to the health and vibrancy of newspapers and the communities they serve. This book is the proof of that proposition.

—*Maura Casey and Michael Zuzel, February 2001*

Table of Contents

PREFACE

By Francis L. Partsch

In the beginning, wrote the Evangelist John, was the Word. If he had been writing about our craft, he would have added, "And the Word was mostly opinion."

For many centuries, journalism was synonymous with opinion—the literary criticism of Defoe and Johnson, the political pamphleteering of Paine and Franklin, the crusading of Beecher and Bryan. Not until the nineteenth century was a substantial wall erected between the two: news on the one side, opinion on the other. By the latter part of the twentieth century, those on the opinion side had come to see themselves as practitioners of a unique and essential craft.

Now a new century is dawning. It's worth asking what constitutes institutional opinion and how it might be most effectively presented and prepared. That's why the National Conference of Editorial Writers and the Scripps Howard Foundation undertook *Beyond Argument: A Handbook for Editorial Writers.*

The book recognizes certain realities. For one, a good many editorial writers enter the craft suddenly and without formal preparation—in some cases because some respected journalism schools still don't teach editorial writing. Indeed, not everyone in academia holds institutional opinion to be a legitimate part of the profession. The literature supporting our craft is surprisingly thin—an indication, perhaps, that most of the people who know enough to speak authoritatively on the subject are all written-out by the end of the day.

Kenneth Rystrom deserves credit for keeping in print the standard college textbook on the subject, *The Why, Who and How of the Editorial Page.* An additional mother lode of professional counsel and inspiration is available from the back issues of *The Masthead*, NCEW's quarterly journal. Furthermore, in the past few years, an NCEW e-mail forum has facilitated wide-ranging discussions among members on a variety of topics, some with startling immediacy. In one instance, a discussion revealed a campaign to plant an advocacy letter in newspapers across the country,

About the author

Francis L. Partsch

Francis L. Partsch has been editorial page editor of the *Omaha World-Herald* since 1982 and before that was the newspaper's state capital bureau chief in Lincoln for six years. He also edited the three-day-a-week *Sidney Telegraph* in Nebraska from 1972 to 1976 and was a staff reporter for *The Wall Street Journal* from 1970 to 1972.

in each instance purporting to be signed by a local reader. The discussion commenced so quickly that some editors still had time to kill the letter.

But none of these sources of information eliminates the need for a "best practices" book such as this. Chapter after chapter offers nuggets that professionals, particularly, can benefit from revisiting or, indeed, discovering, while newcomers can use them as an introduction to a fascinating and rewarding way of life. Nancy Q. Keefe's chapter on time management speaks to any stage of a career. Just about anything by Pulitzer Prize winner Paul Greenberg is worth reading. Ron Clark's views on the editorial page as a community forum deserve the attention of newspaper people from any circulation category.

Underlying almost every word of this book are a couple of hard realities. First, as the division and distinction between news and editorial developed, the line was not drawn down the middle. My newspaper has twenty-five newspeople for every person on the editorial page staff. A similar imbalance exists at most newspapers and broadcasting outlets, regardless of their overall size. The lopsidedness realistically reflects the proportion of the product accounted for by the two types of content. It also invites discussion: Is the opinion arm of the industry given the resources it needs to properly account for itself? Regrettably, that discussion is better suited to another forum.

Second, the news/opinion barrier is porous. Some editorial pages take delight in the breaking of news. Indeed, the machinery of opinion presentation sometimes serves as a newsroom of last resort, supplying perspective—and yes, detail—that the newsroom in its haste may have omitted. Longtime *Boston Globe* editor Thomas Winship, in his keynote speech to the 1990 NCEW convention, challenged us with the proposition that "editorial writers are our last best hope to re-energize the press." At a time when, he said, news managers have become bean-counters and reporters are "snoozing along, dressing well and resting their legs," editorial writers need to stay brave, angry, dogged, outspoken and compassionate.

More problematical than news on the editorial page is the amount of opinion that appears in the sections of the newspaper traditionally reserved for news. Sports columns, city columns and point-of-view feature stories appear throughout our pages. Talk shows fill vast segments of the broadcast day. Even much of what is packaged as hard news these days is not as opinion-free as it ought to be. Adding the pure and unevaluated opinion of ideological journals, advocacy campaigns and of course the Internet raises legitimate questions as to whether print and broadcast editorializing, as we have known it, will continue to play an important role.

Other factors affect the state of our craft. Chain ownership distances the proprietorship from the opinion-preparation function. The prototypical editor/owners who present the editorial page as the institutionalization of their personal philosophy are scarcer these days. In many shops, an editorial board has emerged as the developer and presenter of institutional positions. Other papers have editors who supervise both the newsroom and the editorial page. Still others have editors and publishers who report separately to group headquarters, never treading on each other's territory. Some still have enlightened, aggressive publishers. Some others have de facto independent editorial pages or operate with the publisher only rarely exerting an influence.

Some of these issues, and many others, are touched upon in the volume at hand.

A word of caution to newcomers and casual readers: Don't be dismayed if you find contradictions within these covers. The methodology and underlying philosophy, both in print and broadcast, do not demand the precision of biological science. Different approaches coexist within our assembly, clashing even on such basic questions as the proper structure of an editorial. Do you state the opinion up front and then develop it? Or do you start with the facts and premises and proceed with an orderly argument culminating with the opinion? Any reading of the great editorials of the twentieth century will show examples of both approaches, and others, used effectively. The most fortunate writer works in a shop where all the tools are available, each to be used when it best fits the task.

Considerable discussion has been devoted to the future. Some of us NCEW members argue strenuously that opinion preparers and presenters will have to become more visible in our communities, even to the point of signing our work and opening the policy-formation process to public scrutiny. Others of us maintain that the Ivory Tower tradition serves us well by reinforcing the fact that an institutional opinion is different from an opinion column. The greater innovative spirit is sometimes evident among the smaller and middle-sized shops—such things as editorial-free Saturdays and "community representatives" on editorial boards.

But this is not to say that innovation is hands-down the preferred course. From decades of observation of the leaders of our industry—*The New York Times* and *The Wall Street Journal,* among a handful of others—practitioners should have little doubt that keeping faith with the fundamentals of our craft is the tried and true route to survival. Flashy Web sites and exercises in public journalism might increase our reach, but without clear thinking and effective writing, they are no better than a melodious score with lyrics of gibberish or platitude.

It comes to this: To survive, we must enhance our product by being ever more useful to the consumer. We can best do that by having something of value to say—and by saying it effectively.

The seers in our occupational family have pinpointed the need to accommodate technology, to utilize the potential of online communications and research. That grows, of course, from the need to deliver our product effectively.

However, without in any way minimizing the importance of that imperative, I'd like to look ahead in a different direction. The social and political debates of the time are conducted increasingly with a dearth of stipulated fact and a paucity of common ground. Debate consists mostly of competing assertions, each louder and more vehement than the other. Nearly every social and political point of view has its corps of think tanks and public relations firms, with faxes spinning the news sometimes in the same cycle. In a world in which appeals to emotionalism and ideology are the accepted form of argumentation, it's hard to find the kind of civil discourse that consists of laying out premises, looking for common ground and then identifying, analyzing and perhaps reconciling differences en route to a compromise.

Academia, sad to say, has been co-opted for the fray. Experts, often complete with solid academic credentials, can be found to buttress almost any point of view. "Expert witnesses" appear on the stand to take both sides of the argument in environmental, malpractice and product liability cases. The creationists have recovered from their post-Scopes battering and now have scientists of their own, arguing that Darwin was a fool. And let no one underestimate them: They are not refuted by derisively clobbering them with Menckenisms. They will demand that you publish their pseudoscientific rebuttal, the demolition of which is sometimes beyond the scientific literacy of the average journalist.

Someone needs to keep the public discourse from straying too far. If our craft is going to survive and play more than a decorative role in our respective institutions—as well as bring some order and precision to the public marketplace of ideas—we must have the intellectual wherewithal to get beyond the facade of propaganda and grasp the essence of the issues.

Wrapping ourselves in unexamined ideology, whether that of the left or the right or the greens or the libertarians, is not going to cut it. Today's readers, listeners and viewers demand documentation and logic. Our younger brothers and sisters in this field, to say nothing of our children and grandchildren, will need to know enough science to rebut the glib propagandists, enough theology to sensibly evaluate the pope's latest pronouncement and enough about military life to write about "don't ask, don't tell" without sounding like a total ninny. We need to think long and hard about how we and our successors will prepare ourselves to meet these challenges.

I say we do it starting with mastery of the fundamentals: clear thinking and bright writing. I join my NCEW colleagues in fervently hoping that *Beyond Argument: A Handbook for Editorial Writers* will help point the way.

Chapter 1

Reporting the Editorial

By Jay Bookman

Dead heroes are better than live heroes. For one thing, they're more dependable. They're not going to end up in prison or get caught messing around with a White House intern.

My own hero is the late I.F. Stone, who died in 1989. I first ran across his work years ago, shortly after I started editorial writing, and he's been my role model ever since. Reading his stuff, some of it now almost a half-century old, is still a revelation.

Stone, a free-lance journalist based in Washington, D.C., sold his work on a subscription basis to readers all over the country. At its peak, *I.F. Stone's Weekly* had a paid circulation of seventy thousand, a readership that comprised much of the country's political and intellectual elite. On his office wall, Stone kept an uncashed check for

About the author

Jay Bookman

Jay Bookman has been writing editorials since 1982, winning the National Headliner Award in 1998 and the Walker Stone Award in 1995. He has worked at newspapers in Massachusetts, Nevada and Washington state, and is now associate editorial page editor and columnist for *The Atlanta Constitution*.

Chapter 1
Reporting the Editorial

five dollars, the subscription fee from Albert Einstein.

What made Stone unique was his independence and clarity of thought. He began his letter in 1953, in an era when ideology had blinded millions of Americans, both left and right, to what was really going on around them. Many of his journalistic colleagues also had taken up sides in that struggle, but Stone was able to avoid that pitfall. He certainly had a point of view: As a socialist in the Eisenhower era, it did not go unnoticed. But while his ideology informed his work, it did not dominate it. His writing reads as if he were writing with the benefit of twenty years of hindsight.

In fact, on a long list of controversial topics—Joseph McCarthy, the despotic nature of the Soviet Union, the Eisenhower presidency, Richard Nixon—history eventually came to validate many of the conclusions and analyses that Stone was offering his readers in real time.

I recently lent my collection of Stone's columns *(The Haunted Fifties: A Nonconformist History of Our Times* by I.F. Stone, Little Brown & Co.) to a friend of mine, a reporter who was making the transition to editorial writing. The book was my way of welcoming David to the guild, so to speak. A few weeks later, I happened to ask him whether he had read any of it. Right away, he started marveling at Stone's uncanny ability to cut to the core of things, to understand and then explain what was happening.

Reliable sources

On international issues, *Foreign Policy* magazine, published six times a year by the Council on Foreign Relations, offers a sober, well-informed look at every aspect of international relations, from North America to Micronesia. Articles are written by academics and diplomatic professionals. An annual subscription for $44 is available by writing *Foreign Affairs*, P.O. Box 420235, Palm Coast FL 32142-0235.

"You know how I think he did it?" he said. "The guy was a reporter. He saw things himself. He went to the meetings, he talked to people, he read the documents."

And of course, as soon as he said it, I realized that David was right. In fact Stone, who had been a reporter and editorial writer before going into business on his own, had outlined his method in the foreword to that book.

"I made no claim to inside stuff—obviously a radical reporter in those days had few pipelines into the government," Stone wrote. "I tried to give information which could be documented so the reader could check it for himself. I tried to dig the truth out of hearings, official transcripts and government documents, and to be as accurate as possible."

I think of Stone as an early practitioner of modern editorial writing. To appreciate what that means, it might be useful to look back at the history of the craft.

Editorial writing is perhaps the oldest form of newspaper journalism, and in some ways the least altered by time. Well into the twentieth century, a newspaper typically championed a particular point of view, even in the news columns. That began to change with the spread of chain ownership, one-newspaper towns and a growing sense of professional pride in journalism. Reporters were expected to offer

Reporting the Editorial

straight and unbiased accounts of the day's events, leaving opinion and ideology as the province of columnists and the editorial page.

Even so, editorial writers for a long time basically acted as paid mouthpieces for whatever ideology the publisher supported.

"It was really a different era," said John Bersia, a Pulitzer Prize-winning editorial writer for the *Orlando Sentinel.* "Before we became a Tribune paper [in 1967], our owner and editor would use the paper to push his own personal agenda, with front-page editorials and the whole thing."

Today, most editorial boards still abide by a general ideology, but it is rarely as harsh and hidebound as in previous eras. Following the example of Stone, editorial writers are more likely to rely on good reporting and honest analysis to form their opinions.

For example, Keven Ann Willey, editorial page editor of *The Arizona Republic,* said that, like the *Orlando Sentinel's,* her editorial board in recent years has attempted to move away from a stern ideological consistency.

"I feel very strongly that yes, edit boards can have and should have an ideology. But you have to be willing to test your case, test your perspective, by reporting," Willey said. "We've really worked hard on that. You have to be honest enough to change your perspective depending on what you find."

The importance of that change has been compounded by the new media age. In a world of increasing complexity, at a time when readers are drowning in a flood of confusing and often contradictory information, editorial pages and opinion writing can become the readers' beacon in cutting through that "data smog."

After all, opinion writers presumably have been hired because they are skilled and experienced in consuming and processing large amounts of information. And while the average reader consumes information in this new environment almost casually, in the process of handling myriad other demands on his time and attention, the opinion writer consumes and processes data as a full-time job.

But where does that information come from?

Glad you asked.

Reviewing basic reporting skills in a chapter on editorial writing would be futile, and probably unnecessary as well. Most editorial writers have at least some experience as reporters, and those who do not probably should turn elsewhere for that instruction.

I would, however, like to tackle three more achievable goals. I want to stress the importance of reporting, even when the time constraints inherent in the business would seem to make that impossible. I'd like to talk about the ways in which reporting for an editorial is different from reporting for the news pages. And I'd like to explore the differences, if any, between reporting for an editorial about a local or state topic and reporting on national or international issues.

Let's talk about time first. There's a popular perception that editorial

Reliable sources

Global Connections fox.rollins.edu/~tlairson/gc/links .html), an extensive collection of Internet links to sites ranging from Amnesty International to the United Nations, is an excellent portal to information on foreign affairs.

Reporting the Editorial

writers sit up in their ivory tower, contemplate the events of the day and then eventually rouse themselves to write something. The reality is quite different.

"When we run people through the editorial board from the newsroom, they always come away impressed by the amount of work we do," Bersia said, before reeling off his own duties: five or six editorials a week, a column or Q&A a week, perhaps a more in-depth analysis piece every month or so and two or three public appearances a week.

As Bersia's account demonstrates, many editorial writers produce as many column inches of copy as most reporters on the staff. At smaller papers, they also handle a range of other tasks, such as selecting and editing letters to the editor and designing and proofing pages.

The act of actually writing an editorial is also more time-consuming than writing most news stories. News stories, for the most part, follow a formula. The facts may change, the topics may change, but the basic inverted-pyramid format does not. An editorial, on the other hand, is more like an essay than a news story. It demands more creativity, which often requires more time.

In many cases, however, good reporting can actually ease your time crunch. If you spend two hours listening to the debate in a city council meeting, you've accomplished most

---

Reliable sources

On transportation, suburban sprawl, highway safety and related issues, the Texas Transportation Institute (www.tti.org), an offshoot of Texas A&M University, is a great source both of analysis and raw data about transportation issues, including traffic congestion, mass transit, land-use planning, highway design and construction and pedestrian safety.

---

of your preparation work, and done so more efficiently than trying to track people down by telephone the next day and recreating what happened. Furthermore, during those inevitable slow periods in the meeting, you'll often find time to write much of your piece in your notebook or laptop.

"One three-hour meeting can give you enough material for two or three editorials," said Bernard Stein, editor of *The Riverdale Press,* a weekly newspaper in the Bronx, New York. Stein won the 1998 Pulitzer Prize for editorial writing.

In "Field of Warblers," an editorial in Stein's Pulitzer-winning portfolio, the editor wrote about a patch of city ground used as a stopover by warblers on their annual migration route. A local biology teacher had studied the warblers for years.

"I took just fifteen or twenty minutes to go there and walk around that place, and it entirely changed the editorial," Stein said. "It turned out that it wasn't a pretty place, or some kind of shiny Eden. It had abandoned tennis courts, with trees growing up through chain-link fence. That visit gave that piece life, because I could talk about what it looked like."

Seeing it yourself or depending on the description of others is the difference between writing a movie review after seeing the movie yourself or trying to review the movie sight unseen, based solely on the accounts of others

---

Chapter 1
Reporting the Editorial

Reliable sources

Most newspaper coverage of the Supreme Court, including what's available on the wires, offers at best a cursory look at some of the most important and controversial issues to be decided by government. By the time reporters have explained the basics of a particular case and quoted from the majority and minority opinions, they don't have space or time to delve into its true consequences. *Preview of U.S. Supreme Court Cases*, published in eight issues by the American Bar Association, is a wonderful way to deepen your understanding of the issues before the Court. It offers evenhanded analysis by constitutional scholars, lays out the background facts, discusses the competing arguments, traces the judicial history of the case and relevant precedents and assesses the potential significance of each case accepted by the justices. It even includes a list of those filing amicus briefs in each case and the telephone numbers of lead attorneys. Selected articles are available free online (www.nytimes.com/library/politics/scotus/aba-preview-index.html). A subscription is $130, available from the American Bar Association/Division for Public Education, 541 N. Fairbanks Court, Mail Station 15.3, Chicago IL 60611-3314.

who have seen it. If you witness it yourself, you'll write with more confidence, which in most cases means that you'll write more quickly, and certainly with more authority.

"It's all time management," Bersia said. "At the very least, I try to touch base with a critic, a supporter and someone neutral on every editorial. It's better to have too much research than not enough. When I start to write, I like to have enough material to be writing two or three editorials."

Willey echoed the importance of time management. She and her editorial board adopt a set of issues as priorities each year. Then she tries to free up time for her writers to delve into those topics and make themselves experts.

"Right now, we've got one writer detached for two weeks for reporting on a major piece about growth, which is one of our priorities this year," she said. That can put a strain on other members of her staff, who have to take up the slack. But that kind of in-depth reporting can inform not just the next editorial, but a whole string of editorials yet to come on the topic.

Few editorial writers, however, have shared Bersia's experience with an editorial series entitled "Fleeced in Florida."

"This has been my life for the past year and a half, the most intensive reporting project of my career," Bersia said.

A couple of years ago, Bersia became curious about businesses opening up in Central Florida offering high-interest loans to those unable to qualify for standard credit. When he looked into it, he said, he found that some of the companies were engaged in what he calls predatory lending, charging effective annual interest rates of two hundred, three hundred or even four hundred percent.

A short series of editorials on the topic in January 1999 drew a strong public response, Bersia said, "so our editor told us to do it again, but bigger, bolder, better—his three favorite words."

The series became a crusade, producing more than one hundred editorials on predatory lending practices and eventually forcing a change in public policy. Although the Florida Legislature declined to outlaw the practice, Florida counties and cities, armed with a quirk in state law, began to pass local legisla-

Reporting the Editorial

tion limiting annual interest rates on loans.

Eventually, the *Sentinel* started running a map, showing which cities and counties had passed reform legislation, and which had not. According to Bersia, the map itself eventually became an effective lobbying tool of sorts, used to pressure local politicians to confront the issue.

The effort won Bersia the 2000 Pulitzer Prize for editorial writing.

Any discussion of reporting the editorial has to begin with a decision about your purpose. A reporter is trying to accurately portray the events in question and—on issues of controversy—to reflect the various viewpoints. An editorial writer such as Bersia would approach the reporting task very differently, because his purpose is different.

A reporter is not trying to reach a conclusion. He's trying to present an unbiased account of events, probably complete with a quote from each side, and he can often accomplish that task without having to fully comprehend all the ins and outs of the issue.

That's how a police reporter can walk into a zoning meeting cold, without any background, and still write a competent story: The vote was 4-2 to approve the rezoning; the opponents said this; the supporters said that; the final decision is now up to the county commission. It's not his business to try to determine whether the zoning decision was wise.

The editorial writer, however, is hunting more elusive game. His goal is to understand what's going on, so he can explain it to others. The responsibility is greater, but so is the amount of freedom he enjoys in how he does his job.

Stein knows the difference well, because as editor of a weekly he wears both hats on a regular basis.

"I'm not just an editor or an editorial writer. I have to be a reporter, too," he said. "We have a news staff of five people and me, which means I'm writing front-page news stories as well as editorials."

"As a reporter, I actively went through a mental process of pushing opinions aside," recalled Willey, who worked for eighteen years as a reporter covering everything from local school boards and planning commissions to the police beat, the state legislature and presidential campaigns. "But with an editorial you usually go into it with a perspective. What you're doing with your reporting is testing that perspective, that preconception, against what you find out there."

So, given that difference in goals, how do you approach a source for information? Because he's not looking for news or even quotes for attribution, an editorial writer can offer a source the chance to go off the record more easily than a reporter can.

"My goal in reporting for an editorial is to check my opinions with people whom I respect, who have some

---

Reliable sources

The Rand Institute (*Rand* is an acronym for "research and development") is a private, nonprofit and nonideological think tank headquartered in California. Begun as a government-financed research center specializing in defense issues, Rand has since broadened its work to include a wide range of national issues, from education to crime to the environment. Its free Web site (www.rand.org/publications/) has a database of reports and studies searchable by topic.

Reporting the Editorial

special knowledge," Stein said. "I use them to guide me, and what they tell me is very important even though their names won't appear in the editorial, and what they say is not going to be in the editorial. I'm not looking for information I can quote; I'm looking for a sense of whether I'm on the right track."

Stein cited his work on a recent editorial as an example.

"We've got a situation now where the chairman of the Democratic Party in the Bronx has come out against a sitting congressman, which is unprecedented and I think a disgrace," Stein said. "So I'm making phone calls, but the political insiders who know anything about what's going on aren't going to talk to me if their name is going to be used."

Willey also acknowledged the need for off-the-record conversations, but she's a little more reluctant to grant it.

"I don't offer to go off the record," she said. "I make them ask for it. But once they do ask, I'm usually quicker to say OK than I was as a reporter."

The ability to go off the record often makes reporting for an editorial much easier and productive than reporting for a news story. A distrusting source, wary of being quoted or even misquoted, can be quickly disarmed with a simple promise: "I'm not

Reliable sources

An often indispensable source of information is *Congressional Quarterly,* which publishes *CQ Weekly,* a weekly report on committee votes, floor debate and other events in Congress; and *CQ Researcher,* a weekly intensive look at a single national or international issues. Both publications are extremely useful, but *CQ Researcher* has a special place in my heart. During those slow news periods when nothing much is going on and that editorial space is staring at you like a hungry puppy demanding to be filled, perusing back issues of *CQ Researcher* often can remind you of a topic you have unfairly neglected for some reason. Both publications are also available via the Internet—for those who possess the secret password. For subscription information on either the Web or print version, call *CQ* at (800) 432-2250, ext. 279.

going to quote you. I don't even have to use your name in this editorial. I just want you to explain this stuff to me, because I want to understand it."

In most cases, sources will jump at the chance to try to push their points of view. At the end of the interview, if a particular quote stands out, ask for permission to use it. Most of the time, if the source feels he has had an honest chance to explain himself, he'll usually grant that request.

It's important to make another distinction as well, between the demands of reporting an editorial on a local or state issue and reporting an editorial on a national or international issue. For the most part, they require two different approaches.

Local issues, of course, offer the chance for reporting of a much more personal nature. You'll talk to people face to face, attend the meetings, get people on the phone. The people you're writing about will be reading what you wrote, and they're likely to care about your take on things. As Bersia noted about his series on predatory lending, what you write on local issues is also much more likely to have an impact, for better or worse, on the quality of life of your community and on the reputation of your newspaper.

On local issues, falling back on ideology isn't going to work. Your readers know local issues more intimately than they know national or interna-

Reporting the Editorial

tional topics, and they're going to expect practical, workable approaches that only solid reporting can provide.

Another obvious difference is access. You can call the mayor to talk about his proposal to raise the millage rate to pay for roads and bridges. But unless you write for *The New York Times*, you'll have a hard time getting hold of the secretary of state to talk about the situation in Bosnia.

"There's no question. It's easier to get local people on the phone, and it's easier to go see something for yourself," Willey said. "On national and international topics you're usually depending on secondary sources."

A third difference is the level of reader knowledge about national and international topics. It's a dirty little secret in editorial writing: You can safely write a piece about Afghanistan knowing that, unless you have a strong Afghani community in your readership area, your grasp of the facts probably won't be challenged. Given the deadline pressure inherent in newspaper work, that makes it tempting to skimp on the reporting that you devote to editorials on national and international topics. Just read a wire story or two on the latest development and write the piece.

Reliable sources

• The General Accounting Office, the investigative arm of Congress, is another great source of nonpartisan analysis and data. Its work is also available free on the Web and accessible through a searchable database (www.gao.gov). The same is true of the Congressional Budget Office (www.cbo.gov).

• Science and technology issues are becoming more and more important in public debate, and the National Academies—the National Academy of Sciences, the National Academy of Engineering, the Institute of Medicine and the National Research Council—are a credible source of straightforward analysis on those topics. The academy, like the Rand Institute, is a private organization that performs most of its work under contract from the federal government. Its Web site (www.nas.edu/) has a searchable database of research reports and even a downloadable collection of fifteen hundred books on scientific and technological topics.

However, the idea that such editorials don't need to be reported is false. If you're doing your job well—if you want to bring more information to the thought process than your readers can—then reporting is essential.

But how and when you do that reporting are important.

Realistically, you'll get most of your information and understanding on national and international topics through reading. And if you do most of that reading beforehand—from books, magazines, the Internet, wire services, other newspapers—you'll create a foundation of knowledge to build upon when the assignment comes to tackle a particular topic.

"You name it, I read it: Novels, government reports, the encyclopedia. . . ." Stein said.

However, when the assignment comes, a foundation of general knowledge often isn't good enough. Where do you turn?

Personally, I've become wary of most of the so-called "think tanks," and especially any "studies" they produce. For the most part, groups such as The Heritage Foundation, the Violence Policy Center, the Cato Institute and similar organizations do not take an honest look at an issue; their reports consist

Chapter 1
Reporting the Editorial

of facts twisted to meet the needs of the ideology they serve. In the marketplace of ideas, they are niche producers, obligated by their funding sources to advocate one narrow philosophy or approach. They might be useful as indicators of how partisan debate is taking shape, but as sources of credible information and unbiased analysis, they leave a lot to be desired.

Fortunately, other sources do offer nonpartisan, nonideological analysis on a variety of topics. You won't agree with everything you read from these folks, but the work is generally professional and straightforward, with no discernible ax-grinding.

Bersia has an unusual background that he uses to his advantage. He came to editorial writing after a career in government and public policy, doing graduate work at Georgetown University and American University, and serving as a low-level official in the Carter administration.

He also works with a local Orlando group, Global Connections, that he helped to found. The group sponsors forums, speeches and panel discussions on foreign-policy issues. "We get hundreds of people out for our events, which dispels the notion that people aren't interested in international affairs," Bersia said. That gives him contacts and access to people in government and in think tanks whom he knows and trusts.

Thanks to the Internet, journalists around the country now have access to a vast number of what historians would call primary documents: reports, studies, legislation, court rulings, transcripts and other information. As always with the Web, you've got to be careful about your sources. You've got to know what's real and what's doctored, what can be trusted and what cannot. But reading a news story—or even a dozen news stories—about a new Government Accounting Office report on the F-22 Advanced Fighter program is a far cry from reading the report itself.

The reporter writing a story about the GAO report is looking for different information than the editorial writer, and will cull different information out of the document. What he takes to be the lead, you as an editorial writer may judge to be relatively unimportant.

Most important, you have to bring more to your editorial than just what's already been reported. If all you're doing is regurgitating the same news stories that the reader has already seen elsewhere, you're not going to tell him much he doesn't know.

The Internet is useful in another way as well. Before tackling a new topic, I'll often spend some time roaming through Internet newsgroups, which are discussion boards on everything from the Grateful Dead to evolution to alpine skiing. While you can't necessarily put much credence in the factual information you find in the newsgroups, the participants often will point the way to Web sites that do carry useful documents.

The biggest benefit in reading a specialty newsgroup is the sense you get of eavesdropping on a heated debate among people who care passionately about an issue and are often very well informed about it. You get an idea of how an issue is being perceived, what the fault lines are in public opinion, what misconceptions

Reporting the Editorial

might be clouding the discussion. You might even find that you've had a misconception or two of your own about the topic in question.

So when do you know when you've done enough reporting and are ready to sit and write your editorial? Too often, the clock on the wall will make that decision for you. It's a dictator that can't be resisted.

On too many occasions, however, I've thought myself ready to write a piece and made a last phone call, only to learn something in that call that significantly alters the editorial I would have written. And I'm haunted by the knowledge that on more editorials than I'll ever realize, deadlines loomed and that last call didn't get made.

"I've had that experience too, when you learn something after an editorial is already in the paper and you say to yourself, 'I wish I had known that before.'" Stein said. "And there may even have been a time or two that some information I learned later might have changed my mind."

One of the best signs that you're ready to write comes when you've talked to all of the various parties in a controversy, and you realize that you now know the issue better than any of the participants. It's like the old parable about the six blind men touching the elephant: Each of them knows his own little piece of the elephant, but none sees the whole picture. Only you know that it's an elephant.

Stein, however, has his own method.

"When I hang up the phone and am itching to get to the keyboard, that's a real good sign for me," he said.

Chapter 2

We the people

Framing the Argument

By George B. Pyle

An argument is:

"A coherent series of reasons offered."

—*Webster's New Collegiate Dictionary*

"No it isn't."

—*Monty Python's Flying Circus*

An editorial is an argument.

Not, at least not necessarily, the bang-the-table or smash-the-crockery kind of argument, but the kind that uses logic, example, tradition, emotion, satire, outrage or ebullience to build a case that something should or should not be done.

Or should or should not have been done. Or celebrated. Or rebuked. Just as the word *rhetoric,* which once meant "the art of speaking or writing effectively" (Webster's), has come to mean a lot of hot air that serves no purpose, the word *argument,* which used to mean "a connected series of statements to establish a definite proposition" (Python's), has come to mean an angry exchange of unenlightening contradiction.

The argument found in a good editorial does not take the readers on as opponents to bash, but engages them as equals to converse with. It seeks to convince the undecided, to reassure the ally and to rat-

About the author

George B. Pyle

George B. Pyle is a columnist and editorial writer for *The Salina Journal* in Kansas. He was a finalist for the Pulitzer Prize for Editorial Writing in 1998 and a winner of the Eugene C. Pulliam Fellowship for Editorial Writers from the Society of Professional Journalists. He was once dubbed "that lefty Louie" by Senator Bob Dole.

Framing the Argument

tle the confidence of the opponent.

The means of doing this is very different from the kind of writing found on the front pages of most American newspapers. While the straight news story treats both writer and reader as neutral parties interested in gathering facts, the good editorial is unashamed in its advocacy of a certain philosophy and a certain position.

There are two reasons to do this, two reasons why it is not a betrayal of a newspaper's duty to its readers, or a radio or television station's responsibility to its community, to take firm positions on issues of public concern.

First, institutions devoted to informing the citizens of a community about what has gone on around them have the obligation to go the final step and lay out their ideas of what ought to happen.

Second, Western culture has long accepted that the best way to find the truth is to stage an argument—debate in the legislature, motions and arguments in court—to sharpen and engage the minds of those who must decide.

Editorials can stimulate readers, listeners and viewers to think, to ponder, to learn more—if only to refute what the editorial has said—and to become better citizens, even if they disagree with the editorials. The play's the thing, Hamlet said, in which we'll trap the conscience of the king.

Take a stand

Most good editorials seek action. They urge Congress, the state legislature, the mayor, the electorate, parents, teachers, landowners, dog owners, cell-phone users, taxpayers, renters, students or the community as a whole to do something. Or not do something. And editorials should give reasons why. They may not have space for the twenty-seven specific reasons for action cited in the Declaration of Independence, but the why of any proposed course of action, given specifically and forcefully, is the difference between a restated news story and a good editorial argument.

Note how the Pulitzer Board describes its criteria for awarding the top prize in this craft: "For distinguished editorial writing, the test of excellence being clearness of style, moral purpose, sound reasoning and the power to influence public opinion in what the writer conceives to be the right direction."

The Inland Press Association also bestows an annual award for what it considers the best editorials.

"Criteria for judging the quality of editorials," Inland says, "are:

"Clarity of thought

"Pungency of phrase

"Statement of a need or expectation in concrete terms as a basis for action

"Fostering appreciation of humanity's limitations, capability for folly, and potential for glory."

Editors agree.

"A good editorial makes a clear case, a persuasive case," said Dick Benfield, editorial page editor of *The Record* in Hackensack, New Jersey. "A good editorial produces some action."

Or, perhaps, stops it.

Although phrases such as "cau-

Framing the Argument

tion is called for" are ridiculed as examples of editorials that wimp out, it is also possible that the argument an editorial will make is that some action being contemplated, even one with widespread support, is a foolish course of action.

Just because the train has left the station, said Van Cavett, retired editorial page editor of the *Allentown Daily Call* in Pennsylvania, doesn't mean the engineer knows where he's going.

John Nichols is editorial page editor of *The Capital Times* in Madison, Wisconsin. He says that one purpose of editorials is to stimulate readers to argue important issues in their own lives, with special help given to those who agree with the newspaper's point of view.

"This is a way to reach out and engage people," Nichols said. "We give people ammunition for when they are sitting at the bar."

Like *The Capital Times*, founded and maintained as a progressive publication rooted in Wisconsin's reform movements, the *St. Louis Post-Dispatch* editorial page lives by a credo, set down by founder Joseph Pulitzer, that supports the working person and opposes the concentration of power. Making a difference, not just making arguments, is a goal these editorial pages share.

Christine Bertelson, editorial page editor of the *Post-Dispatch*, explains that editorials in her newspaper are written to move people, to get action out of public officials or the electorate as a whole.

The point of any editorial, Bertelson said, is to address a specific issue and call for a specific action on the part of a specific person or body.

The process of writing every editorial starts out with an understanding of whom the argument will be aimed at and what result is desired.

"Our editorials will come right out and say, 'Here's what you need to do, Mr. Mayor,' or 'Here's what you need to do, health department.' The point is to accomplish something. That's what we're here to do," said Bertelson.

She feels the *Post-Dispatch* accomplished something in the state's 1999 statewide ballot initiative to allow Missourians to carry concealed weapons. The newspaper opposed the idea, early and often.

"We really cranked it up," Bertelson said. "The good guys won because of historic voter turnout in our readership area. That surprised even us."

For those efforts, *Post-Dispatch* editorial writer Philip Kennicott was nominated for a Pulitzer Prize for what the judges called "his carefully reasoned editorial campaign."

The democratic dialectic

Of course, not every editorial can make a difference. Some, perhaps, don't want to. Some may see it as some sort of an abuse of power for the largest community forums in what are, these days, almost exclusively one-newspaper towns, to push events in the direction they want.

But that's no excuse for wishy-washy or timid editorials. For one thing, perhaps the only belief more arrogant than the assumption that a newspaper should convince people to think certain ideas and act in certain

Chapter 2
Framing the Argument

ways is the assumption that it can.

Minds may not be changed. But they may be opened, and people may at least rearrange their prejudices a little.

"A good editorial gives people who don't have a firm opinion, or who have the opposite opinion, a reason to think," said *The Record's* Dick Benfield.

"A good editorial will at least open their minds to your point of view."

On many subjects, many people may not know what they think. New issues appear. Important ones are ignored. Just pushing an issue to the top of the public's list is a valuable public service.

Jay Ambrose writes editorials for Scripps Howard News Service. Though he believes in fiery, passionate editorials, he doesn't see them as the answer so much as a particularly useful way to put the question.

"Democracies accomplish things through a kind of a dialectic," Ambrose said. "The process itself has a lot of value."

The newspaper as a whole, of course, carries many other voices besides the editorial board's. Rare is the newspaper that gives ink to only one side of a debate. Even an editorial that states a clear argument for or against something is as likely to enrage as to convince, as likely to inspire the other side to marshal its arguments, sharpen its statistics and field its advocates.

An editorial should put its argument, its position, plainly before the reader. In Ambrose's case, that usually means in fewer than four hundred words, with the editorial's opinion coming at the beginning, the middle and the end. Then—we hope—the readers' or listeners' own minds take over, he said. Even if the editorial does not win agreement from any of its readers, it may well have caused them to think about an issue. It may be an issue the readers or listeners have never thought about before, or one that has been relegated to a long-time prejudice that has never been questioned.

If they think about it, think about it some more, and then decide that the editorial is wrong, well, that's the breaks. And, Ambrose said, the readers and listeners will be better off for having gone through the exercise. "I think of editorials as being part of the conversation. In a democracy, every citizen, even editorial writers, should be part of the conversation."

Bernard Stein, editor of *The Riverdale Press* in New York City, won the 1998 Pulitzer Prize for editorials on a variety of local topics. He likes people to agree with him, but that's not the only measure of success for an editorial.

"I hope readers will start arguing with me in their heads," Stein said. "Yes, I'd like to change people's minds. But what's important is that they hold whatever opinion they hold intelligently, hold it as something they have thought about."

Unlike the author of a straight news story, who may feel obligated to include the wide range of pros and cons, an editorial writer is in a position to bore in on the most important angle.

"A good editorial frames the issue," said Tommy Denton, editorial page editor of *The Roanoke Times* in Virginia. "Focus is critical. Focus on the core of your thesis."

Framing the Argument

Denton points out that the editorial writer has limited space, and the editorial reader limited time. That's why most newspapers' editorials are relatively brief, and the best ones go quickly about their business arguing that something should be done, or stopped, or at least explored.

"You've got to use a scalpel and some small-bore arguments," Denton said. "And put some lemon pepper in there from time to time."

The passion play

The accomplished editorial writers whose brains were picked for this essay come from different parts of the country, are arrayed on many different points along the ideological spectrum and write editorials that range from brief bullets to expansive essays. But all agreed on one thing.

A really good editorial must be felt as well as thought. The 2000 Pulitzer Prize for editorial writing went to John C. Bersia of the *Orlando Sentinel*, "for his passionate editorial campaign attacking predatory lending practices in the state, which prompted changes in local lending regulations."

If an editorial is unconvincing, not thought-provoking or just plain dull, it does not fulfill either the public-spirited mission of improving one's community or the more private goal of selling lots of newspapers. And such failures, Van Cavett pointed out, come not from lack of technical skill on the writer's part but from a lack of passion. A lack of passion, he said, does not protect the writer from the reader's contempt, it only makes the reader wonder why he bothered, and why he should care.

"You have to write with some conviction about the issue," Cavett said. "Couch it in such terms that the reader will say, 'This is someone who knows what he or she is writing about. I may disagree, but I can see their opinion and see some reason behind it.'"

Ambrose, of Scripps Howard, agrees. "For them [editorials] to be meaningful, there has to be a sense of passion," Ambrose said. "Not that every one has to be all fiery. You have to hit the tone that's appropriate to the topic."

Roanoke's Tommy Denton notes that passion is necessary to make an impact. "A good editorial always strives to present a cogent argument that not only is persuasive but also pulses with some metabolism," Denton said. "You don't have much time or space. You're working on the head and the gut."

This emotion, of course, need not be anger or excitement. It can be sadness, pity, joy or contempt. An editorial calling for additional safety regulations can thunder about greedy manufacturers, or it can condemn the sloth of government regulators.

But when an issue is illustrated by relating the death of a child in an auto accident, or because of an unfenced swimming pool, grief is probably the appropriate emotion. Dragging out a dead child, even for the best of causes, must be done with respect for the dead and concern for the feelings of loved ones. In such a case, sadness is the appropriate emotion. Public figures, of course, are fair game for criticism and, sometimes, even ridicule. But if the point of the editorial is to

Framing the Argument

move public opinion, it can be counterproductive to publicly wound someone on the other side and win him widespread sympathy.

"Be merciless in terms of argumentation, but not in terms of personalities," said Paul Greenberg, Pulitzer-winning editorial page editor for the *Arkansas Democrat-Gazette.*

Don Gale wrote and delivered editorials on KSL radio and TV in Salt Lake City for twenty years. He believes in stating a firm, clear opinion, but warns editorial writers to stay away from anything that might be taken as an attack on someone's character or a cheap shot. "To be too strident is a mistake," Gale said. "It turns people off." Such a concern is particularly true in the broadcast media, as words that can appear firm and direct in print can seem downright mean when a face or a voice delivers them. "So many people forget that the credibility of an editorial page is not something that is earned in a day," Gale said. "If you sacrifice that credibility by being too strident, it will take a long time to build it back."

There is no rule that all editorials must, as the cliché goes, view with alarm. Sometimes, good things happen. And the editorial writer who wants to be allowed to share the community's grief, outrage or offense also must share in its joy. So rave about the public arts fair or the youth mentoring program. Celebrate the restoration of the old railroad station or the drop in teen-age pregnancies. Praise the public official who kept a promise or who resigned rather than prolong a divisive feud. Note, with a sense of loss, the passing of a public

figure or community activist, even one you disagreed with. Especially one you disagreed with.

Frank Partsch is editorial page editor of the *Omaha World-Herald.* He urges editorial writers to take on different topics and search out fresh angles. "There are an awful lot of editorial writers, and an awful lot of editorial pages, that I don't really care to read because I already know what they are going to say," Partsch said. "I like to have a new wrinkle or a good story."

So welcome summer. Be in awe of romance. Marvel at the powers of nature. Garrison Keillor, host of "A Prairie Home Companion," has been heard to object to the East Coast media's habit of saying the Midwest was "paralyzed" by a blizzard.

Why not, Keillor asked, say that the Great Plains were "mesmerized" by the falling snow, so entranced by the sight of it all that many hundreds of poems were written in Iowa alone? Editorials in that vein can keep the writing gears lubricated and keep readers from thinking they can predict, after a glance at the front page, what the editorial writers will be on about today.

Finding your voice

Greenberg—or was it Mozart?—has often said that a work should include just as many notes as are required, no more and no less. Greenberg's fellow Pulitzer winner Bernard Stein knows he is swimming upstream when he says this, but he says it anyway: "Most editorials are too short. They become kind of a grunt, something like, 'I like peanut butter,' or 'I don't like peanut butter.'" It is important for the topic to be

Chapter 2
Framing the Argument

given the style and number of words it deserves. Stein said his editorials frequently run from six hundred fifty to eight hundred words, though he has also been known to indulge in doggerel poetry and other, briefer forms when appropriate. Gale, whose editorials were heard rather than read, figured out that if he wrote editorials of exactly two hundred forty-seven words, that would fill the ninety seconds he had to make his point. He found it a helpful way to force himself to organize his thoughts, focus on one or two points and make them clearly. (The Gettysburg Address, just by the way, is two hundred seventy-two words. We are told it took three minutes to deliver, counting five interruptions of applause.) "The secret to writing is organization," Gale said, "how the words flow and how people can almost anticipate where you are going."

Just the number of words in an editorial is not a measure of its burden on the reader. Even a long editorial made of short, declarative sentences can be easily digested.

It is a matter of rewriting and revising. Omaha's Frank Partsch said: "Sometimes I get done with a piece and then go get a bag of periods and go back through it. Almost any piece can benefit from a few shorter sentences."

I didn't realize I was using this device until a professor of journalism pointed it out. After a long sentence or paragraph I thought necessary to convey a complex idea, I nearly always add a very short paragraph—perhaps no more than "Well" or "You don't say?" or "What bunk"—just to give the reader a chance to catch up.

If the Pulitzer Prize for Editorial Writing is any guide, some of the best editorial writing is done by individuals at small newspapers—Greenberg, then at Pine Bluff, Arkansas; Stein at the family-owned weekly *Riverdale Press;* Michael Gartner in Ames, Iowa. In 1998, when Stein was the Pulitzer winner, the other two finalists were Clint Talbott of the *Colorado Daily* in Boulder, and me of Salina, Kansas. That year, the judges described Stein's work as "graceful," Talbott's as "powerful" and mine as "insightful." Stein, Talbott and I made up a discussion panel at the 1998 NCEW convention in Ottawa, Canada. We noted that each of us had the freedom to write what interested and moved us, without the need to first convince other members of an editorial board. And we all had the space to write editorials of whatever length we thought necessary. Panel moderator Phil Haslanger, managing editor of *The Capital Times* in Madison, Wisconsin, instantly dubbed this phenomenon, "Room but no board." Such a situation makes it rather easy for the small newspaper's editorial voice to be consistent. Larger newspapers with editorial boards may actually have a more difficult time keeping a clear voice. The challenge there is for the editorials to avoid the tone of having been written by a committee—even if they were.

Admirers of Paul Greenberg's *Arkansas Democrat-Gazette* note that the longer essays in that newspaper's editorial slot, which remind some of us of the "Talk of the Town" pieces that lead off *The New Yorker* magazine, carry a consistent voice that gives the impression that they were all written by a single person—even

Chapter 2
Framing the Argument

though they weren't. (Of course, *The New Yorker* "Talk" pieces are now signed, and no longer carry the unified style they once did.)

That is where a clear mission, such as those of *The Capital Times* or *St. Louis Post-Dispatch*, can help. *The Capital Times'* John Nichols says his newspaper's unwavering progressive stance helps it keep a principled consistency. Not only does that help the editorials stick to the newspaper's values, but it also allows the editorial writers use of those values as a scale to measure the words and action of politicians. "The absence of an ideological grounding is what has made a lot of editorial writing unentertaining and uninteresting," said Nichols. He dismisses as "fantasy" the whole idea of an impartial newspaper.

When a paper like *The Capital Times* is hard on Democrats who fall short of progressive values—or a paper like the *Arkansas Democrat-Gazette* is hard on Republicans who fall short of conservative values—it gives a newspaper the kind of independence from partisanship that both enhances the newspaper's credibility and improves its ability to raise the level of debate.

On the other hand

The old newspaper joke is about the editor who was looking for a one-armed editorial writer, one who would never say, "On the other hand. . . ."

Noting the opposing, or one of the opposing, arguments to an editorial's point of view may be the least a writer can do, out of fairness and in order to build his own case.

"You have to give a fair shake to the other point of view," says *The*

Record's Benfield. "Editorials aren't supposed to be objective. They are supposed to be fair."

Noting the other side, at least in passing, buys the editorial credibility and strengthens its argument. It lets the reader know that the other side has been considered by the editorial writer and has been found wanting. Madison's John Nichols says noting the opposing view can be key to an effective editorial.

"We acknowledge the opposite view, and then we seek to destroy it," Nichols said.

Arkansas' Greenberg cites H.L. Mencken, who recommended attacking the strongest argument of the opposition. Remember, though, that it is still an argument we are building here, not a list.

Van Cavett stresses that it is a waste of time for the writer, and the reader, when an editorial simply and dispassionately lays out the reasons on both sides of a case and then says, for no apparent reason, *"The Daily Blow* believes. . . ."

If you haven't built the case for why *The Daily Blow* believes it, there is no reason anybody else should care.

Sublime to the ridiculous

Sometimes, something happens that is just too delicious for an editorial writer to avoid commenting on, even if it is not a matter of public policy or the opportunity to influence anything has passed. Here at *The Salina Journal*, we have been known to damn with faint praise, or to feign confusion at the goof-ups and misjudgments of our local officials. We have even been known to

Framing the Argument

thank local officials for an obvious misdeed, on the grounds of giving us lonely scribes something to write about.

Such was the case when the Salina schools banned the Star of David from posters advertising a high school production of *The Diary of Anne Frank* on the grounds that it had become a gang sign. We called it an obvious easy target offered to the newspaper in return for its years of support for public education.

And when a middle school principal confiscated all the copies of a student newspaper that questioned the fairness of school disciplinary procedures, we lauded the official for finding a way to encourage literacy among his students: Make it forbidden.

Satire and humor, though, can be a dangerous route for an editorial writer. Omaha's Partsch and New Jersey's Benfield, among others, caution against such trickery unless a writer is particularly skilled at it, or a topic screams for such an approach.

"When you try to do something by indirection," Partsch said, "almost always someone will be confused by it. When you are writing editorials you have to give up some of the tools that a universally educated readership would expect to see."

Driving it home

When *The Salina Journal* was redesigned several years ago, one of the challenges was to make the editorial page more inviting to the casual reader. And one of the devices the designers came up with turned out to assist the content as well as the form. For the benefit of all those too busy to read an entire editorial (mine run around four hundred to five hundred words), two lines were added at the top of every editorial: "The issue" and "The argument." My favorite example of this was "The issue: Electing judges. The argument: Don't." But the fact that these fields have to be filled in for every editorial helps me remember that the editorial has to include an idea that can be so summarized—it has to be about something.

Salt Lake City's Gale said he would close his TV and radio editorials by saying, "KSL believes. . . ." That both reminded his audience that his statements were an institutional opinion and drove home his basic point one last time. News stories often go from here to there, from the beginning of a story to the end. Editorials more often end where they began, stating the argument at the beginning, outlining the reasons and ramifications in the middle and returning to the argument at the end.

An editorial is an argument.

The Crime of Hatred and the Crime of Silence

This editorial criticizes the actions of local government officials but puts most of its emphasis on a call for the entire community to take a stand against racially motivated violence. It was part of the portfolio that won the Pulitzer Prize for Editorial Writing in 1998.

Every day when those of us who are parents say good-bye to our children, a little tooth of anxiety gnaws at us until we see them again. No

Chapter 2
Framing the Argument

matter how old or how mature they are, no matter how confident we are that we have prepared them for the traps the world sets, deep down we fear that something terrible will happen to those we love.

For one family of Riverdalians, the call every parent dreads came last week, when their 17-year-old son was waylaid, threatened, terrified, and humiliated in North Riverdale in broad daylight. The young man wasn't mugged. What happened to him was far worse. He was attacked because of the color of his skin.

A middle-aged white man who claimed to be a police officer stopped the young man on Spencer Avenue by brandishing a gun. He pushed him up against a parked car, forcing him to assume the position of a suspected criminal, and peppered him with questions about what someone who looked like him would be doing in a neighborhood like North Riverdale (the neighborhood where the young man has lived all his life). "If you ever come into this neighborhood again," he threatened, "I'll kill you."

In a cry for justice addressed to Mayor Rudolph Giuliani, the young man's mother asks, "What are the leaders of this city going to do about restoring my son's confidence? What are we supposed to tell him after training him to respect all authority? Our son is a sensitive young man who celebrated the diversity of his community. . . . What do we do for him now? He's afraid to walk in his own neighborhood."

Three and a half years ago, hoodlums assaulted a group of young Orthodox Jewish students at the 235th Street overpass, taunting them with epithets. Hundreds of residents flocked to a rally organized by Rabbi Avi Weiss of the Hebrew Institute two days later. Mayor David Dinkins dispatched the city's Human Rights Commissioner to express his concern. Borough President Fernando Ferrer, Councilwoman June Eisland, two members of the State Assembly, and representatives of Congressman Eliot Engel and mayoral candidate Rudolph Giuliani spoke. The clergy turned out in a body. The entire community made its revulsion at bigotry clear.

By contrast, virtual silence has greeted last week's incident. Councilwoman June Eisland and Assemblyman Jeffrey Dinowitz have contacted the family and expressed their outrage. After the young man's mother followed up her letter with a phone call, Bronx Borough President Fernando Ferrer's office called back. But at press time, nine days after the victim's mother appealed to the Mayor, neither he nor his police commissioner have responded. And no other community leader has come forward to voice concern or compassion.

As a community, we need to answer the young man's mother's questions. We need to assure her son that he is welcome here. We need to promise him that we won't assume a black man must be up to no good. In our homes and schools, we need to tell his story to our children, so that they'll understand that racism is not a phenomenon of America's past but a present threat to our own lives.

The thugs who assaulted this

Framing the Argument

young man insulted all of us. They assumed we would applaud what they did, or at least regard it with indifference. Don't let our silence prove them right.

—Bernard Stein
The Riverdale Press

A Brave New World

This editorial is an example of how not every editorial attacks wrongdoing or calls for action. Still, it is an argument, an argument about the very nature of the universe and how it should be seen. It was part of the portfolio that was nominated for the Pulitzer Prize for editorial writing in 1998.

Did you feel it? Last Thursday? Nothing much, perhaps. The world just came to an end.

For the first time in 150 years, members of two bands of Kickapoo Indians, divided by time, war, wanderlust and forced migration, met at the Kickapoo Reservation in Kansas.

The significance of such a meeting is clear from the fact that, a century and a half ago, a spiritual leader of the Kansas Kickapoo called Kenekuk the Prophet foretold that its occurrence would presage the end of the world. And so it did.

For the world ends every day. And it begins.

People are born. They grow up. They move. They marry. They move again. They die. Others are born.

Old friends drift apart. Families reunite.

The Earth turns, moves through space, changes. Our perceptions of that Earth are altered by time, science, faith, experience, disaster and triumph. The prophecy was well known to the many Kickapoo, to the band that has lived in Kansas since 1833 and the band that has lived in Texas and Mexico nearly as long. It was known enough to, as Harris News Service reporter Mike Shields reported last week, cause some concern among those taking part in the reunion.

Too respectful of their own heritage to simply reject the prophecy, some of the Kickapoo applied the modern practice of looking for loopholes. They noted that there are not many full-blood Kickapoo any more, so a foretelling of what happens to Kickapoo no longer holds. But there is no need to reject this prophecy, or any other prophecy of any other belief system, or to add footnotes. And there is no need to envision earthquakes, tidal waves and fiery volcanic eruptions as part of any world-ending scenario.

The world ended Thursday for the Kickapoo in the sense that a long separation had ended. The world also ended Thursday for maybe a billion other souls, who saw something about the world they knew change forever. It is the stubborn clinging to the old world, and the fear of the new, that keeps Jew hating Arab, Protestant fighting Catholic, Hutu killing Tutsi, black mistrusting white,

Framing the Argument

woman tiring of man, child fearing adult. Somewhere, the world comes to an end every day, every minute. That is good as often as it is bad.

And Kenekuk the Prophet, like many other prophets, deserves credit for his vision.

—George B. Pyle
The Salina Journal

FRAMING THE ARGUMENT

Writing: Making It Sing

By Paul Greenberg

Of all the ways to write better editorials, one is my particular favorite. Perhaps because it's a pleasure. Perhaps because it has to do with what is most missing in editorials: an ear for language and the sound of a human voice.

It's this: "Read poetry. It doesn't matter what kind. Pick your own favorite—good, bad or indifferent, Longfellow or Emily Dickinson or Seamus Heaney. But read poetry."

Read it aloud, the way you should be able to hear your own editorials in your mind and ear as you write. One of my favorites is a twelve-line poem of Seamus Heaney's called "Squarings." It's about building a cottage, but no writer need be told that it's not about building just a cottage. Read it aloud. Slowly:

Squarings

Roof it again. Batten down. Dig in.

Drink out of tin. Know the scullery cold.

A latch, a door-bar, forged tongs and a grate.

Touch the crossbeam, drive iron in a wall,

Hang a line to verify the plumb

From lintel, coping stone and chimney-breast.

Relocate the bedrock in the

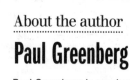

About the author

Paul Greenberg

Paul Greenberg is a columnist for the Tribune Media syndicate and editorial page editor of the *Arkansas Democrat-Gazette*. An editorial writer for more than thirty years, he has won numerous awards for editorial writing, including the Pulitzer Prize for Editorial Writing and the Scripps Howard Foundation's Walker Stone Award. He was a Pulitzer finalist in 1978 and 1986.

Writing: Making It Sing

threshold.

*Take squarings from the
recessed gable pane.*

*Make your study the unre-
garded floor.*

*Sink every impulse like a bolt.
Secure*

*The bastion of sensation. Do
not waver*

*Into language. Do not waver
in it.*

So many editorials one sees, but never finishes reading, waver. Until they waver away. The editorials do not read well because they are not written well. And they are not written well because they are not thought out well. The writer does not know his tools, his words. Impulses fly, thoughts are unplumbed, there is no iron and no wall to drive it into, facts are missing, and matters are not squared. Words and phrases are called on to cover all the gaps in thought, like wallpaper applied with one hand—in a hurry, under deadline, without care. You can see, you can feel, the bumps and crinkles and cracks that weren't supposed to show. The writer has supposed that his job was to manipulate words, not think thoughts. And it shows. Lewis

Carroll's advice has been forgotten: Mind the thoughts, and the words will take care of themselves.

It's always a surprise when the words spring magically to mind—usually after we've spent a lot of time and effort thinking about a subject, growing familiar with it, living with it, learning its parts and plumbing, following its lines without wavering. No, none of that may show in the editorial. None of it should show. But all of it will be evident. The editorial will have a sense of authority, discovery, conviction. It will have a natural eloquence, sometimes homespun, sometimes elegant, but always there. Think of how it is with a great teacher or a great chef, whether their style is closer to Julia Child's or Adlai Stevenson's.

"The best editorials," said Hap Cawood, retired editorial page editor of the *Dayton Daily News* in Ohio, "come from a resonant feeling about an issue or event—surprise, interest, horror, anger, humor—plus a confidence in yourself to express your reaction well. At your best, three elements work together: The news, your reasoning power, and the insight beyond your conscious mind."

It takes practice, like any other sport, but so often we spend our time doing everything but writing. Because most of us, whatever we tell

---

A word about broadcast editorials . . .

Editorials written to be broadcast should be addressed to the ear, too, and to the eye if they're written for television. They need to be just as good, only shorter. Or rather more concise. Remember that these editorials may be heard and seen, or just overheard, by folks who are driving or cooking supper at the time. So the broadcast editorial needs to be succinct, strong, and clear. It needs to sound simple even when making a complicated point. The writer's words will have to emerge from the background radiation of life to catch and hold the listener.

Writing: Making It Sing

ourselves, will do almost anything to get out of writing. Edit the columnists. Work the letters. Play computer games. Actually answer all that e-mail. Attend meetings. Talk about writing, even write about writing. And of course read, but always call it research.

You know the story about the writer whose husband took the kids and left her alone for the day so she could finish her column. He came back in the evening to find that she'd polished every piece of silver in the house.

One of the things I do to put off writing is to draw up lists of ways to write. I'm up to forty-two, and more occur to me even as I write this piece. But technique isn't writing. It may have been Raymond Carver, the short-story writer, who said that, when a writer starts talking about technique, you know he's fresh out of ideas. There are plenty of techniques. Not a one can take the place of an idea, any more than form can substitute for substance.

Archy the Cockroach had it right. He used to come out at night to ghost-write a column for Don Marquis of the old *New York Sun*. And this is what Archy told Don in one of his columns:

boss i am disappointed in
some of your readers they
are always asking how does
archy work the shift so as to get a

new line or how does archy do
this or do that they
are always interested in technical
details when the main question is
whether the stuff is
literature or not

A word about broadcast editorials . . .

The potential for powerful editorials in the electronic media has scarcely been touched. Too often these editorials consist of more talking heads talking, and the visual power of television is scarcely used. It's a mistake to use video for the sake of video, but the right picture at the right time, like the right word in a sentence, is a thing of beauty and conviction.

The best writing comes from some emotional spur. It comes from the solar plexus, or maybe the liver, or gallbladder. There is an elation in reasoning, too—as when mathematicians speak of an elegant solution. By all means, reason. Writers who don't are going to find themselves in trouble, but reason can come later in the process. Write with feeling, edit with reason.

Perhaps the best thing an editorial writer can do for his readers is take his time. Time's the stuff writing's made of. Or at least the illusion of time. We've got to be able to sit down to write with the feeling that we've got all the time in the world to say something that needs to be said now. The urgency should come from the subject, not the clock. It's essential that time be set aside for writing—several hours a day in which you don't do anything but work on your editorial.

Ideas need time to gestate. A writer, somebody once said, is a person who lets no experience go unused. Somebody was wrong. An editorial writer needs to be as selective as he is retentive. Or he'll wind up writing a diary, not an editorial. And

Writing: Making It Sing

you have to be a John Cheever or Samuel Pepys to make a diary interesting.

You don't have to write during the time you've reserved for writing—but make it a rule not to do anything else. Not to answer letters or do "research," or surf the 'Net, or pay bills or polish the family silver. Just sit there and stare at the screen if you have to, but don't do anything else but write. Eventually you will. You'll be driven to it out of desperation. The psychiatrists call it writing behavior.

And never show a work in progress. Many a good editorial has been talked away before it was written. Phil Geyelin, who used to write a column for *The Washington Post,* once told me that the political column was a dying art form. You'd never know it from the proliferation of columns today. Now it's the editorial that's dying. It needs reviving—before the columnists completely fill the vacuum we're leaving. Because they're the ones now meeting the demand for strong, forthright, interesting opinion with a human voice. There's no good reason editorials can't meet all those requirements, although plenty of excuses are offered.

The first thing that needs to go, after the excuses, is those daily editorial conferences. They're boring as Hell and twice as long. Do you know of any painter or sculptor or real writer who would invite in a roomful of colleagues to tell him how to proceed? Isn't that the function of the editorial confer-

---

A word about broadcast editorials . . .

To write and deliver an editorial for television requires more than non-glare glasses and clear diction, although those are good starting points. The temptation to dumb down editorials must be resisted, and the challenge to make editorials compete with the best on the air gratefully accepted.

---

ence? Even if we call it policy-making, as if this were a foreign ministry instead of an editorial page. Maybe that's why so many editorials read like committee reports. Because that's what they are. Because we're aiming for consensus, not opinion.

Think about it: Has anything good ever been written by committee? (Don't mention exceptions like the King James Bible and the Constitution of the United States, both of which were miracles.)

We forget what a free form editorials can be. The man who is tired of London, said Doctor Johnson, is tired of life. I don't know about London, but anyone tired of writing editorials is tired of life—or has confused editorials with the fixed, static, ponderous kind that no one actually reads. We're handed whole columns of empty space every day, like an empty canvas, and told to fill it. It ought to be perfect freedom. Richard Aregood, editorial page editor of *The Star-Ledger* in Newark, New Jersey, remembers his reaction when that first happened to him at the *Philadelphia Daily News:*

"Scary as it was, there was the opportunity to look at that two-column drop every day as an art form open to whatever I did with it. So the *Daily News* editorials became an odd mix of one-line jokes, outraged rants and the occasional essay that built like an essay rather than a newspaper story. Too often, we start thinking of an editorial as a limited thing that has

Writing: Making It Sing

to take the same shape every day, not realizing that the readers are more than willing to follow us into whatever stylistic alleyways that make the point best. For the more sports-inclined, it's the way an aging pitcher has to think, mixing the pitches continuously for maximum effect. Some issues demand a fastball on the fists; others need a knuckleball."

That's the kind of realization editorial writers need to hold onto. Especially when we find ourselves slipping into a routine solemnity. Why confine humor to "humorous" editorials? Humor makes a better condiment than it does a whole dish. Ask anybody who ever had to read one of those humorous editorials that aren't. It's like being unable to get away from a bad comic.

It helps to write to the ear, not the eye. Every writer has a personal style, or several, and should. The easiest to read is the conversational. An editorial should be addressed to the individual reader, not the public, or the world in general. It should be a letter to your Aunt Matilda or to Angry Young Man, not To Whom It May Concern. And it should say something, which sounds easier than it is.

A writer named Sholem Aleichem—he was dubbed the Yiddish Mark Twain—toured this country at the turn of the nineteenth century, and he would often start his presenta-

---

A word about broadcast editorials . . .

The editorial writer who's starting out in radio or television has a lot of good examples—and tapes—to learn from. Consult the work of pioneers like Don Gale in Salt Lake City (now a life member of the National Conference of Editorial Writers) or Dave Ross of CBS Radio. The styles of broadcast editorials can be just as varied as those in print, from direct and businesslike to tongue-in-cheek. Don't forget to have fun.

---

tion by saying: "Before I begin speaking, I'd like to say something."

We ought to sit down not to write an editorial but to say something. Instead of editorializing, or columnizing, or lecturing, we ought to say something. And not waver. If we don't have anything to say, let's not say it. Let's leave the space blank, maybe with a small line reading: Compliments of a Friend. It'd be a big improvement.

A piece of opinion ought to have one. It shouldn't be just a restatement of the obvious. It ought to go to a second level of interpretation—beyond the common, immediate reaction to the day's news. Readers can be trusted to have their own instinctive reactions to the news. They don't need us for that. They should be able to look to us for something more—for some mental traction. What's an editorial anyway, but the day's news after somebody's had a chance to think about it?

Resolve here and now never to write another editorial about Unfunded Federal Mandates, or Infrastructure Needs. Remember that language should have verve—and verbs, too, especially in headlines. And that editorials can also praise. To quote Catherine Ford, columnist for the *Calgary Herald* in Alberta, Canada, "Great editorial writers are known for the skill of their criticism, but also for their praise, praise being by far more difficult to do well."

Chapter 3
Writing: Making It Sing

And edit, edit, edit. Then have the final product edited by another pair of eyes, another human sensibility. (The general sign of good editing is that the piece grows shorter, not longer.) An editorial writer who winds up editing his own stuff is in the same predicament as the lawyer who has himself as a client.

It helps to have read a bit of your favorite opinionator before you sit down to write—H.L. Mencken, William Allen White, Grover C. Hall Jr., G.K. Chesterton, Rebecca West, Florence King, George Orwell. . . . Whoever yours is, re-read a paragraph or two before setting out on an editorial. We all learn to write by imitation; why not mimic the best?

Aim for a masterpiece every time. The great thing about this business is, you come up to bat every day. Why settle for the routine, the dutiful, the grounder to second? Swing for the fences. Wouldn't you much rather read a really unabashed, outrageous, atrocious, dead-wrong piece of opinion than one so safe, so predictable, that it lacks . . . opinion?

Forget the kind of opinion that's really something else—news, analysis, pro-and-con, or an ill-fated attempt to resurrect Walter Lippmann. There's a reason the signature phrase of the editorial writer has become "On the other hand. . . ." Don't just avoid the phrase—avoid that whole, unopinionated approach to opinion.

Editorials are the heart and soul of a newspaper; they give the paper a character of its own apart from the news it reports. The editorials in a reader's paper should share his sense of place. It's a sad thing to pick up an editorial and not be able to tell, from the local references and the local twists of speech, what part of the country it comes from. Our editorials should have a sense of identity, and bolster our readers'. One of the better if apocryphal mottoes for a newspaper is supposed to have adorned one in Buckley, West Virginia, years ago: "The Only Newspaper in the World That Gives a Damn About Buckley."

And don't forget that you can tell a story. The narrative may be the best and the most neglected form of the editorial.

We've got the grandest job in the world, as Grover Hall reminded us all in a classic editorial headlined "Dull Gulls." And if we haven't enjoyed writing an editorial, the reader isn't likely to enjoy reading it. Or to stick with it for very long.

What all of us want to do is write great, penetrating, life-changing words . . . and what we're expected to do is to please just not embarrass the paper. Certainly not by writing anything that would upset people, or reveal ourselves. The result: One day we wake up and wonder if, after all our training and experience, we can still write.

Gustave Flaubert could have been singing the editorial writer's blues when he wrote what has become my favorite plaint about the inadequacy of language: "Human speech is like a cracked kettle on which we tap out tunes for bears to dánce to, while we long to make music that will melt the stars." We have to believe that we can melt the stars—in the very next editorial.

There was a time—during the nineteenth century, mostly—when it was

Chapter 3
Writing: Making It Sing

not considered in bad taste for an American editorial to take risks, to pronounce upon the issues of the day or even of the ages without wavering in conviction—or language. Those editorials did not hesitate to reveal a mind at work or even a mind at play.

People talked about those editorials. Because they were worth talking about. And even acting on. Having your newspaper censored, or your printing plant burned down, may be the sincerest of compliments. Having an infuriated speaker at a whites-only rally in little Pine Bluff, Arkansas, back in the bad old days hold up a copy of your editorial and rip it to shreds to the roar of the mob . . . that beat any Pulitzer. Such protests are a testimonial to the power of the written word, and proof that we haven't forgotten how to invoke it.

Who would bother ripping up an editorial today? The biggest problem with the American editorial page today is that it consists largely of editorials. Not thoughts or feelings or opinion—except of the more predictable kind in the more predictable kind of prose.

Today's editorial page oozes prudence, which is too often a euphemism for fear, especially the fear of ideas. It's usually not fear of what our editor or publisher might think. That's the least of it. But fear of what our own oh-so-respectable selves might think. So is self-censorship born. And mediocrity. Respectability has ruined more editorial writers than drink ever did.

Of course the editorial writer should avoid embarrassing his newspaper, but that should be the beginning of our work, not the end of it. A terrible fog of calculation seems to hang over our editorials—a fear that events may prove us wrong. Or that, if we go back to first principles and think them through, we will sound, well, unconventional.

So we write to cover every eventuality and contingency, stretching the language beyond the bounds of elasticity or even meaning, and may scarcely notice when the language snaps under us, or just goes limp. And we wonder why people no longer read editorials. Don't they know it's their duty? Alas, we've made it a duty, not a joy.

Our job description is Editorial Writer. And we've been so intent on the first word that we've just about forgotten the second. Most of us begin as frustrated politicians anyway, as statesmen manqué, and we're so busy second-guessing the real ones that we forget we're supposed to be writers, not politicos.

H.L. Mencken is a much better guide. A writer, said Mencken, "is a man in whom the normal vanity of all men in so vastly exaggerated that he finds it a sheer impossibility to hold it in. His overpowering impulse is to gyrate before his fellow man, flapping his wings and emitting defiant yells. This being forbidden by the police of all civilized countries, he takes it out by putting his yells on paper. Such is the thing called self-expression."

The editorial writer, man or woman, boy or girl, has to learn how to commit this kind of craziness in workmanlike prose. Like any other art, it involves a helluva lot of just plain work. Though it's only when it feels like work, instead of the best stuff you've ever written, that you

Writing: Making It Sing

know it's a lost cause. Too many editorials sound as if they were written by people who are biding their time until they get a column of their own, so they can really start to write.

The editorial writer who knows his subject, who follows it and reads after it, who has a genuine and continuing interest in it, and even some cherished prejudices about it that he's developed over the years, will be prepared when it makes the news. Chances are he'll also be prepared to stretch the bounds of his subject, and, in writing about it, to say something about the human condition. He may even be surprised, or shocked, or delighted, or appalled, or enlightened by the news, and be able to communicate that to the reader. That is the mark of a great editorial.

The editorial writer who stays interested in the world about him will find that the world stays interested in what he has to say about it. That's why the writer needs to come to his subject with a well-stocked mind, and with much more: with unique, personal feelings and memories ready to be triggered by the news of the day. To dare

put all of that together in the editorial column of a newspaper requires a strong ego, but luckily editorial writers are seldom short in that department.

Sometimes I finish an editorial and feel like leaning back and applauding. Sometimes I do applaud. It tends to startle the people out in the newsroom. Of course sometimes I boo and hiss, too, and hit the delete key. (Would I had deleted more.)

Even realizing that you've written an unpublishable editorial is better than churning out the standard, inoffensive, carefully qualified and perfectly safe editorial that barely editorializes. Call it the editorial-lite. Surely that's not why we became editorial writers. But we forget. We are lulled by Editorial Enemy No. 1: routine, habit, all the reflexive responses we've fallen into after having written essentially the same editorial about the same subject too many times.

That's not writing, as Truman Capote would say; that's typing. It's turning out editorials when we should be saying things that need saying. Now.

42 Ways to Write an Editorial
By Paul Greenberg

1. Take a line. —H.L. Mencken

2. Don't confine humor to the "humorous" editorials.

3. Shorten and if possible eliminate the editorial conference, where more good ideas have been slaughtered than at the United Nations.

4. Vary style.

5. Use clear, sharp, palpable, tangible references, preferably local ones in local language. Write to the ear, not the eye. Write as you speak. Try a conversational tone. The reader should be able to share not only a sense of sight and sound, but also a sense of place.

6. Thinking about editorials is not a job; it's an avocation, hobby, obsession. Let no good idea escape you.

7. Address the reader directly; don't orate. Picture a particular person—your Aunt Matilda?—when writing.

Chapter 3
Writing: Making It Sing

8. Writing is rewriting.

9. Editing is often rewriting. Approach the editorial with a fresh eye and ear each time. It helps to put some time and space between each rewriting.

10. Write with feeling; edit with reason.

11. Three-quarters of the trick is to pick the right subject—one you feel strongly about, know a lot about, are interested in.

12. Put writing first—before layout, before administration, before editing the columnists or addressing the civic clubs or answering correspondence.

13. Set aside time for writing. Keep that time free even if you just sit there, think, and don't write a word. The easiest thing in the world is to be distracted from writing.

14. Attack the strongest part of your opposition's case, not the weakest. This is sport, not persecution.

15. Never hesitate to run a correction. Even when one may not be altogether necessary. It'll be the best-read item on the page.

16. Be tough on ideas, easy on personalities, silent on people's appearance.

17. Remember that the headline is part of the editorial; pay at least as much attention to writing it as you do your most cherished sentence.

18. Don't sit down to write an editorial, but to say something.

19. Arrange your schedule so that you have an opportunity to review the editorial after it is written or even in type, and to re-review it. Allow time between exposures. Time or the illusion of it is the key to good writing and editing.

20. The best writing comes from some emotional spur.

21. Do not abort editorial ideas in embryo. Write them out fully, then evaluate them. Then they can be seen in full.

22. Go to a Second Level of interpretation and comment, a level beyond the obvious. Don't treat an idea or proposal or event only within its own context, in intellectual isolation. Tie it in with some larger meaning or different perspective. Write the only editorial in the country that will appear from your particular point of view—a product of your unique experience, knowledge, wisdom, viewpoint, crotchets and insights.

23. Offer your reader some mental traction. Use a cartoon instead, if all you can offer the reader is pap. Don't write on a subject for no better reason than that everybody else will.

24. Keep your favorite editorial or writer in mind. Imitation is the most natural form of writing.

25. Aim for a masterpiece, not just another editorial.

26. The completed editorial should be considered a first draft.

27. Use symbols and metaphors that move and affect, not just for the sake of symbolism.

28. Enjoy your work; it'll show.

29. If you must use a cliché or a worn phrase, change it slightly.

30. Forget editorials that are news analysis, background or general mush. Editorials should be opinion. The facts buttressing an editorial should show, like the beams of a well-constructed cabin, but the whole structure should be about opinion.

31. Give local topics top priority. And write about them in a knowledgeable, local way.

32. Never fudge or cheat or lie a little; you'll be glad you didn't.

33. A balanced page of opinion helps.

34. Pay special attention to the letters column. Run letters as soon as you can.

35. Don't forget the narrative style.

Writing: Making it Sing

36. Remember that writing editorials isn't a chore; it can be art, literature, therapy.

37. Don't forget that you've got the grandest job in the world.

38. Call it the Florence King Rule: "A cardinal rule of writing is never interrupt yourself to explain something. If you must bring up an obscure topic, drop informative hints about it as you go along so that you don't end up with the entire explanation all in one place. This keeps you from skidding to a stop and sounding teacherish. Otherwise it's better to omit the obscure topic altogether, or as mothers might put it: If you can't say it interestingly, don't say it at all."

39. "Shed excess baggage, so you don't slow down the camel train. If you care about good writing you omit words that have no meaning, and prefer shorter ones that mean the same thing. When your prose is lugging freight that has nothing to do with the topic and is only put there to register your support of feminism, the outcome is not merely ugly but ludicrous. It reads as if it were pasted with bumper stickers." —David Gelernter

40. "We read to find out what we already know." —V.S. Naipaul, in an essay on Joseph Conrad. "The best editorials articulate what everyone knows but no one has ever said before." — William Allen White.

41. Whenever you're about to repeat the conventional wisdom, phrase, or jargon *(infrastructure, situation, global economy/warming)*, think it through before writing—to see if you're not just lazily writing around a point instead of examining it. Don't sweep uncertainties under the rug, settling for some kind of vague run-around instead of direct speech.

42. Read poetry. It doesn't matter what kind. Pick your favorite—good, bad, or indifferent, whether Longfellow, Emily Dickinson or Seamus Heaney. But read poetry. It trains the ear, revives the soul, enlivens the spirit within prose.

The Editorial Crusade

By Meg Downey

Consider this:

In Florida, the *Orlando Sentinel* documented how growth was out of control and zoning regulations were being ignored, damaging the environment and overwhelming the school systems. The county eventually set a five-year moratorium on urban development in rural areas and waterways were given special protections.

In Connecticut, *The Day* in New London showed how nuclear power plants were cutting operating costs and, as a result, compromising on safety. The Nuclear Regulatory Commission finally shut down the plants.

In Vermont, *The Burlington Free Press* exposed the pollution in the state's supposedly pristine water.

Eventually the state rewrote its standards for water quality.

In Indiana, *The Indianapolis Star* sought to overturn a failed system for teaching children to read.

In New York, the Rochester *Democrat and Chronicle* helped make a high school better, and the *Poughkeepsie Journal* helped forge the creation of the Hudson River Valley Greenway, a plan to guide growth and create a network of parks, trails, historic sites, farms and waterfronts from Manhattan to Albany.

This is the fun stuff—the big caus-

About the author

Meg Downey

Meg Downey is the executive editor of the *Poughkeepsie Journal* and was editorial page editor of the *Journal* for twelve years. She has won numerous state and national awards for her editorials, including a National Headliner Award, the Scripps Howard Foundation's Edward Meeman Award and the Fourth Estate Award. In 1997 she was a finalist for the Pulitzer Prize for Editorial Writing.

es presented on an editorial page that, when pursued relentlessly, can change the character of a community, can improve people's lives. As editorial writers or broadcasters, you can take a small piece of the world and serve it well. And that can make you love being in this crazy business.

If the news pages of a newspaper feed a community's hunger for information, the editorial page can feed its soul. It should not just reflect a community's character. It should mold it.

And it can often do that best by not leaving investigative reporting to the front page but by presenting the same kind of in-depth research on the editorial page, analyzing the facts and then offering solutions.

Any size staff can do it. Yes, it's harder if there's just one or two of you. But the results are worth it—even if all that's accomplished is getting people to think about something in a new way.

Do the legwork

Make sure your series looks ahead as well as looks back. It should offer possible solutions. For a paper to say its city needs leadership is like saying cows need hay. What about it? Rochester took a different approach to school board elections; rather than just do endorsements, it got ahead of the game and named people it thought should run.

Use database reporting to give readers information. The *Poughkeepsie Journal* offered state test results and graduation statistics for every school district over a five-year period and gave percentage changes. The point was to show that fewer students were taking the tougher state Regents exams and most were graduating by passing minimal requirements, getting the equivalent of an elementary school education.

In 1998 Stephen Kiernan, editorial page editor of *The Burlington Free Press* and winner of the 1999 Best of Gannett Award for his work, spent four days going through every pollution report filed in the state of Vermont. Near the end of the first day he found that fifteen hundred gallons of chlorine used by the state's sole nuclear power plant had been dumped in the Connecticut River, killing many fish, and the state had taken no action. On the second morning he found that a hydroelectric dam reservoir had been lowered well beyond what its permit allowed, killing every fish in the reservoir. Again the state took no action. After four days, the many examples of environmental abuse and state negligence led him to draft the series "Troubled Waters," which looked at how Vermont had fallen behind in enforcing its once-respected water

> **"A country editor**
> is one who reads the newspapers, selects miscellany, writes articles on all subjects, sets type, reads proof, works at the press, folds papers and sometimes carries them, prints jobs, runs errands, cuts and saws wood, works in the garden, talks to all his patrons who call, patiently receives blame for a thousand things that never were and never can be done, gets little money, has scarce time or materials to satisfy hunger or enjoy the quiet of nature's grand restorer, and esteems himself peculiarly happy if he is not assaulted and battered by some unprincipled demagogue."
>
> — *Poughkeepsie Journal*
> In the nineteenth century

Chapter 4
The Editorial Crusade

protection policy.

Look beyond the obvious sources. Kiernan, for instance, talks to people who used to hold leadership positions—former governors or cabinet leaders. "They're never shy about talking about what couldn't get done," he said.

In any campaign, it's important to look past the immediate concerns—to anticipate change. It's much easier to be bold—in your ideas and in your writing—when you're in charge of events rather than responding to them. The *Poughkeepsie Journal* ran a series of editorials on economic development, and, yes, it was important to look at tax breaks and other incentives to draw business to the valley. But the *Journal* also urged state land use reforms to better guide growth and save the region's cities. The paper pushed for international partnerships, notably with the Czech Republic and China, to open up untapped markets for businesses. While everyone was scrambling to attract new high-tech companies to the Hudson Valley, the *Journal* made a case to preserve a strong industry, often ignored, that was already there: agriculture. Farming was not only a big business, it was also a major tourist attraction, and it was the views of farmland that drew many residents to the region in the first place.

And never let an editorial series die. Persistence can be as important as substance. Too often newspapers launch a major campaign on an issue and after some initial success, they drop it. But the poor habits of some people in government will return if newspapers do not keep after them.

Where is an issue in six months, a year, five years? Be vigilant.

The best approach is to develop a follow-up plan before the series even runs. The *Poughkeepsie Journal* ran its series on economic development in advance of a public forum that the paper sponsored with the local community college. The editorials were reprinted and distributed at a forum to which government, business and civic leaders had been invited. Members of the public also could sign up to attend. The forum was covered by both the news and editorial staffs, and a subsequent agenda for change was published on the editorial page based on a consensus of ideas from the forum.

Help readers learn more for themselves. *The Indianapolis Star* ran a four-part series by Andrea Neal exploring how the whole-language system of teaching kids to read had failed in the state. To follow up the series, which won first place for commentary in the 1998 National Awards for Education Reporting, Neal said, "We mailed out more than one hundred copies of a report by Bonita Grossen, 'Thirty Years of Research: What We Know About How Children Learn to Read.'"

Get out of the office

You may get good quotes, you may get information, but you rarely get passion over a telephone. The best reporting and the best writing come from being in the midst of the story.

You can describe the beauty of a valley once seen by Hudson River School artists a century ago if you stand on the same hilltops that they

The Editorial Crusade

did. You can relate the bitterness the elderly feel when forced to sell their highly taxed homes because you interviewed them over bridge and doughnuts at an American Legion hall. You have to visit the places you're writing about.

Great projects come from getting out of the office. James F. Lawrence, award-winning editorial page editor at the *Democrat and Chronicle* in Rochester, New York, happened upon one of his paper's most important editorial campaigns, improving Franklin High School: "The project was actually conceived during my visit to the school for a Career Day. Several teachers and students whispered to me about the school's multitude of problems. After returning to the office, we discussed the pervasiveness of Franklin's problems. I wrote a column for Sunday's paper announcing the project and we've been banging away for nearly three years." Staff members attended PTA meetings, met privately with teachers, students and administrators, and attended special meetings at the school.

Bailey Thomson, associate professor of journalism at the University of Alabama and former associate editor at *The Mobile Register* where he still pitches in during the summer, found that even in 1998 Alabama had fallen behind its neighbors in school reform, children's programs, civic discourse and, yes, in eradicating racism. Thomson spent weeks visiting six states in the Deep South in 1998 and interviewing scores of people. He showed how the positive change he found elsewhere contrasted with Alabama in a series of editorials called "Dixie's Broken Heart." It won the 1999 Distinguished Writing Award for editorials from the American Society of Newspaper Editors. See how his research made his words powerful:

Along U.S. 11 in Tuscaloosa County, which parallels Interstate 59, you pass the back door of Alabama's new Mercedes-Benz plant. Rising Oz-like in the distance, its white buildings shimmer through the native pines, suggesting the wizardry and wealth of Alabama's high-tech dreams.

Go east for another mile or so, and you'll see what appears to be a down-at-the-heels trailer park. Families sometimes stop there to inquire about renting. What they find, however, is Vance Elementary School. You can't see the original building from the road because 17 portable classrooms surround it. . . .

The most effective editorial projects are those that stir the blood. Show passion and compassion, the fist and the heart, and you will make a difference.

How to add depth

Don't just reflect on what's going on in your community. Look for answers elsewhere. Find out how other communities handle major issues. Search on the Web. Talk to national organizations that represent issues you're writing about. For instance, the American Planning Association, based in Washington, D.C., can cite you examples of how different communities have dealt with growth issues, from encouraging public transportation to saving farmland to creating affordable housing. Join NCEW's listserv—the online discussion group of editorial writers—and ask colleagues how their communities have addressed a similar issue. Then go visit and see for yourself. When Neal wrote about reading problems in Indiana, she looked to California where the whole-language system of teaching reading had been eagerly adopted and where it turned into a disaster. She used this failure in the Land of Sunshine to teach her own state a lesson.

The Rochester *Democrat and Chronicle* conducted a campaign to improve the academic quality of a local high school. The paper held four round-table discussions, inviting separate panels of alumni, students, teachers and parents to talk about the school's problems. Excerpts of these discussions were published on the paper's Speaking Out page in its opinion section. Then the paper held a fifth discussion that included one participant from each of the previous roundtables plus the school's new principal and headmaster.

Look at history. Go into your archives and find information and photographs related to your topic. Look back fifty years and show how Main Street was hopping when department stores and fancy restaurants were downtown. Quote from old documents that show how a historic institution, now in decline, was once the centerpiece of its community. Find old studies that looked ahead to the present and predicted what would happen if communities didn't plan well. Local planning departments can be great sources for that.

Show, don't just tell

Howell Raines, editorial page editor of *The New York Times,* said at an NCEW convention in 1991, "I really don't believe in 'eat your peas' journalism where you kind of drag the reader one bloody inch at a time through a body of information." He evoked the premise of the Romantic poets, that "the object of good writing was to inform and to delight."

Good editorial writers do that. Vivid, descriptive writing is essential. Don't tell people why your topic is important; show them. Describe precisely the globs of toxic PCBs emanating from the bed of the Hudson River.

Be specific. *The Hartford Courant* fought to keep Hartford's hockey team, the Whalers, from leaving the city. It didn't just deliver palaver; the paper told readers that Chuck's Steak House would lose up to eight thousand dollars a game night and that Al Franklin's Musical World would lose twenty thousand dollars a year. It made its cause personal.

When Jane Healy, now managing editor of the *Orlando Sentinel,* wrote "Florida's Shame," her Pulitzer Prize-winning editorial series on uncontrolled growth in the 1980s, she looked to persuade readers by continually showing cause and effect. To demonstrate the impact of development, she looked at what happened to the schools. "They would just cram kids in schools," she said. "Kids were having to eat lunch at ten-thirty in the morning and were hungry by three." She also named names and told how people who used to work for the county would influence county commissioners to get their improper develop-

Chapter 4
The Editorial Crusade

ments approved. The tone, Healy said, is important. "Let the situation itself make the argument," she said. "You don't need to be shrill. You don't need to say, 'You should do this.'"

Find the human angle on technical issues. Maura Casey, associate editorial page editor of *The Day*, faced a challenge when she wrote about nuclear plant safety in southeastern Connecticut, which is very comfortable with nuclear power, dominated as it is by a naval submarine base. Casey said, "I chose to personalize the myriad of safety issues through the attempts of whistleblowers to get attention paid to the safety lapses at the plants, and their own struggles as they lost their jobs in retaliation."

Orlando Sentinel editorial writer John Bersia, in a campaign called "Fleeced in Florida" that won the 2000 Pulitzer Prize for editorial writing as well as Scripps Howard's Walker Stone Award for editorial writing, let his stories about people make his point. An excerpt:

> *Whether lawmakers want to admit it or not, Florida has legalized loan sharking.*
>
> *Consider.*
>
> *—A Sanford woman who's now going through a divorce has only her car to her name. She turns to a title-loan company for a paltry $250 loan. In return, she is charged interest and fees totaling 264 percent a year—plus the company keeps an extra set of keys to her car, just in case she doesn't pay up.*
>
> *It's all perfectly legal.*

Have fun with your imagery. The *Portland Press-Herald* in Maine did in an editorial that said: "Mainers' frustration with government is as palpable as the tang of salt air on our coast or the early autumn scarlet now creeping onto our trees."

Word choice is important. Live with a good thesaurus next to you. Neil Heinen, editorial director of WISC-TV in Madison, Wisconsin, said, "I try to use words that sound as good as they read, and read as good as they sound. I try to use words in a way that might surprise the listener and force them to pay attention. And I try to use a combination of short and long sentences that, in total, have a rhythm and flow." Newspaper editorial writers also should read their writing aloud to see if it flows well.

More papers should bring the human voice into the editorial. What rule is there that editorial writers can't use original quotes? Broadcasters often do better at this because they need the audio or video of someone speaking to add substance to their editorial commentary.

Thomas Gray, the seventeenth century poet, once wrote of "thoughts that breathe and words that burn."

That passion must be conveyed from the first sentence. Eloquence can sell ideas. Just about the worst offense we can commit on the editorial page is to be boring.

Use art, graphics and logos

Photographs, illustrations and graphics should be used to emphasize points, bring life to a subject and help readers digest complex information. Use a photograph to show a treasured

The Editorial Crusade

vista that may be lost. Use maps or architectural drawings to define the impact of new development. Show economic trends in charts. Remember that numbers are hard to understand in editorial narrative—on the page or to the ear. Show them in graphic form whenever possible.

The Seattle Times had an idea about how to save the Columbia River salmon. The challenge, editorial writer Lance W. Dickie said, was how to present a solution in what was a complicated morass of issues such as improperly built dams, farming and logging practices, climate, ocean conditions, harvest, predators, hatcheries and the impact of development. The *Times* did it by having graphic artists create a presentation that showed readers how dams work and what changes the paper recommended. It made "a daunting load of copy approachable," Dickie said.

For broadcasters, compelling images are essential. Heinen's station in Madison ran an aggressive campaign in support of construction of a new convention center. "The editorials that were most effective," Heinen said, "were those that showed the construction in progress and dealt with issues of disruption, environmental risk and building design."

Every series should have a name and a logo that runs with each related editorial to help it have impact over time. This tells readers it is important, and they should pay attention. Further, promote the series in advance on the opinion page, in a billboard on the front page and on your newspaper's Web site. When the series runs, include a box outlining all parts of the series—what's coming and what has run.

How to get started

Get up. Look out the window.

To do a big, in-depth project for the editorial page, you need to think first. And how do you get the time to do that? You steal it.

You do it by planning ahead. Editorial boards at many papers and television stations have year-end meetings when they determine the editorial campaigns they will take on in the next year. These usually are long-range issues. WISC-TV in Madison, for instance, looked at three topics in 2000: the emergence of biotechnology as a long-term economic strategy for the state and the University of Wisconsin, opportunities and challenges for people with disabilities and the issues confronting Madison as it grows into a big city.

Pick your topics, then save anything having to do with them: government reports, news stories, public documents, magazine articles, Web sites offering background on different topics, names and numbers of people who are experts in a field. Save this information for years even. It will give you perspective later.

Steal time by deciding how you spend it. On a small staff, it may mean that once every two weeks the daily page is given over to local columnists debating a topic rather than having an editorial that day. Then you can do research on a project instead. Make an appointment with yourself to spend a specific two-hour period each week doing reporting on your

The Editorial Crusade

special project. If you need to read a report or other background material as part of that research, then take your phone off the hook.

Even better, work at home. Take a day off to outline a plan for your project—editorials and topics, accompanying columns to solicit from experts in the field, ways to interact with the public, Web sites and other online initiatives, with deadlines for all. Later, when you're in the midst of it, work at home a day every two weeks to do your major writing. You'll be more efficient without the interruption of phones and meetings.

For projects to be well-planned and well-researched, it's critical that management give its support to editorial writers. That may mean allowing one editorial instead of two to run in order to give an editorial writer time to do reporting on a project. It may mean giving you the time and money to attend a seminar on the topic you want to cover. When Maura Casey at *The Day* was immersed in researching the issue of safety at nuclear plants, she traveled to Tennessee to a Nuclear Regulatory Commission training center to get twenty hours of training in nuclear power.

Small staffs can raid other departments to get help. When Casey was editorial page editor with *The Eagle-Tribune* in Lawrence, Massachusetts, the executive editor had different editors in the newsroom take turns writing an editorial or two once a week, on Thursdays, to lighten her load. "I appreciated the respite," she said, "and the editors looked forward to writing an opinion piece on a topic of their choosing."

Make the case for extra time or help to your editor or publisher by outlining the scope of the project and what its impact could be. Managers who see the potential long-term benefit usually will back up your efforts. And you should help them out, too, because they will bear the consequences of your editorial series. After *The Day* published several particularly hard-hitting editorials about nuclear safety lapses, Casey said, the utilities that owned the nuclear plants took out full-page ads denouncing *The Day's* coverage and editorials. Neither her editor nor her publisher, who took plenty of critical phone calls, "got weak-kneed," then or at any time when she wrote about problems at the nuclear plants, she said. "Partly this is because I would often send them the confidential memos and information upon which I based the editorials so they could be prepared when critics called in."

What do you tell the news side about your project and about information you may find during your research? There's no one answer. Some papers stay completely independent of the news side right down to not having a conversation with news reporters and editors about projects the opinion page is working on.

At the *Poughkeepsie Journal*, the opinion page staff keeps the news desk informed about what it is pursuing, since a news story a reporter is working on could have an impact on the opinion page project. Research done by the opinion page staff is not shared unless it involves a major breaking story that should get into the newspaper. The approach is: How can readers best get this information?

The Editorial Crusade

Get experts, readers involved

Eminent columnist Walter Lippmann once suggested that the role of newspapers should be to "get the community in conversation with itself." A good editorial series—whether in print, on the air or on the Web—should spur public debate. That can be done in many ways: through public forums, expert panels, focus groups, questionnaires, polls. All of this can be done in the paper, in the community or online.

Stephen Kiernan in Burlington said he and the one other editorial writer on his staff develop a list of critical issues. Then they bring in experts on an issue for a roundtable discussion. The session is taped and the transcript typed up so it can be run in segments along with the editorial series. "We'll bring adversaries in the room and watch the energy and friction between them," Kiernan said.

Readers can help develop a project, and your words may influence them all the more if they've had a hand in it from the start. In 1993, the *Poughkeepsie Journal* launched a series called "Charting Change" to develop a plan to help the Hudson Valley fight back from the loss of thousands of IBM jobs. A questionnaire asked readers for their ideas. Four hundred people responded. Their responses were published, and their comments helped shape the series. The *Journal* used anecdotes from readers to help bring home points about the need for better public transportation and improved telecommunications systems. Their quotes brought issues to life. And public officials paid attention to what their constituents were saying. The *Journal*, by

answering their questions, became more important to them.

You can also ask readers what questions they want answered, then ask experts to answer them in a question-and-answer format on the op-ed page.

Tell readers and viewers what they can do to get involved. Run the phone numbers, mail and e-mail addresses of public officials or agencies. Give information about coming meetings on the subject. Tell people how they can obtain public records. Put it all on the Web and refer to Web sites where readers can obtain more background in a subject.

It's also fine to go wild once in a while. After a massive ice storm in Vermont in 1998, Kiernan said *The Burlington Free Press* "created a nonprofit organization, named a board of directors and ran a four-month campaign to remedy the destruction. It raised a pile of money (which later won a federal match), did a bunch of good and culminated in a festival in a city park with music, speeches by local, state and federal officials, a kids' car wash, face painting, a visit by the local pro team mascot, the Army honor guard, tree planting, etc., etc."

Decide when to publish

There's no correct rule here. It depends on the timeliness of the topic. On something that will play out over time, such as zoning or land use issues, one strong editorial presentation a month is enough. Once a month also may be easier to handle for a small staff. Some topics, related to a specific problem involving breaking news—such as how a community should address a threatening source

The Editorial Crusade

of pollution—may better be published during the course of one week. The problem with publishing a series for a number of days in a row is that you can overwhelm the reader with too much information—and you may limit your ability to deal with important editorials on breaking issues unrelated to your project.

However you decide to publish, make sure every editorial is placed online with links established to pertinent Web sites.

Finally, always consider making a reprint of the editorial series. (Remember to save your pages as they're published on your computer pagination system or on disk to make it easy for the copy desk to put them together for a reprint.) The cover page of a reprint should tell why you did the editorial series, summarize what you found and let readers know the reprint includes information telling them how they can act on the issue. Then send the reprint to all the movers and shakers in your area with a letter asking them for their response. That can help prompt them to pay attention, and you can hold them accountable for what they say they will do.

Is all of this effort worth it? Ask Jim Lawrence of Rochester: "It's rewarding to see tangible evidence of change. As a result of the Franklin campaign (a drive to improve a local high school), a blue-ribbon commission of local leaders was appointed to explore new options for the school. The school board later endorsed the panel's recommendations and a fully revamped Franklin High School, with the support of twenty-five million dollars in infrastructure improvements, is being phased in over the next several years."

The editorial page is your pulpit. Use it well.

"To do" list

Within six weeks of publishing your series:

• Have a detailed outline.

• Assign op-ed pieces to experts in the field.

• Solicit readers' ideas on the editorial page and online.

• Begin to outline the steps readers can take to act on the issue.

• Meet with the photo and graphics department to discuss how to present the topic visually.

• Plan the order of publication and whether you will do a reprint of the series. Publish simultaneously on the Web.

• Develop a promotion plan, including advance promos and a front-page billboard the day the series begins. Do the same online.

• Set aside days to work exclusively on the series.

Chapter 4
The Editorial Crusade

Chapter 5

Stretching the Form

By Richard Aregood

Long ago, when I was first viewing with alarm (as all editorial writers are expected to do), a dandelion-haired rookie in the opinionating business and the only person on the *Philadelphia Daily News* editorial page, the boss had an idea he thought was great. He wanted me to write an editorial that properly appreciated the benefits of the death penalty.

Even then, I was a bleeding-heart liberal, albeit one with a frequently altered consciousness. This was something a fine, gentle fellow like me could never write.

Yes I could.

I fled to the little two-person office in which the editorial page hippie shared quarters with the black columnist. (These were the days when one of anything was thought to suffice.) We thought, mulled and joked about how hilarious official murder wasn't.

Suddenly, an evil idea occurred to me. I read a week's worth of my own newspaper. Like any urban tabloid, it detailed the adventures of some truly bad guys, hired killers who not only bumped off the person they were supposed to kill but also whacked anybody who happened to be in range. Suddenly, there appeared a man who would not be missed, a man whom any Western hero would not blink at killing. His name was Leonard Edwards.

About the author

Richard Aregood

Richard Aregood has been editorial page editor of the *Star-Ledger* in Newark, New Jersey, since 1995. He spent twenty-eight years at the *Philadelphia Daily News* in every editorial department save photography, and won the Pulitzer Prize for Editorial Writing in 1985. He is grumpy but basically a fine fellow.

Stretching the Form

So on November 21, 1975, just in time for Thanksgiving, the readers of the *Daily News* got this for breakfast:

Yes, the Chair

It's about time for Leonard Edwards to take the Hot Squat.

Edwards, for those who haven't been following his worthless career, has been convicted of two murders. He's awaiting trial on another murder and the rape of a 14-year-old girl.

He's 29 years old. Hope of rehabilitating this piece of human crud is doubtful. It's even wildly optimistic to use the word doubtful.

The last time Edwards was freed, it was on bail pending appeal of an overly generous third-degree murder conviction. He had just stabbed somebody to death and justice, in all its majesty, had found him guilty.

Edwards then went out and killed somebody else.

His second murder jury was right. He's not worth the upkeep.

Fry him.

Ask any reader which editorials make his eyes glaze over, and you won't hear about the odd ones. The ones that make them nod off are the very same ones that make us nod off in the middle of writing them—the required ones, the ones we feel obliged to do.

The fun ones, those we often think of as throwaways, are often the most invigorating for both the writers and the readers. It is helpful to think of the editorial pages as the equivalent of a self-contained newspaper, one that has the obligation to entertain as well as inform and fulminate. This may not go over very well with publishers and executive editors, many of whom think of what we do as little better than an opportunity for trouble. A nice, stupefying, incomprehensible news story about the sewer board will bring a satisfied smile; an impassioned call for the resignation of its just-indicted chair may not.

But we can prevail. The first step is to look coldly and dispassionately at the personality of the newspaper we work for. That will determine the style of anything we might do to brighten things up. If it is essentially a boring old uncle who occasionally scolds, then what we write must be consistent with that personality. Uncle Ned, in other words, is not likely to get antic, put a lampshade on his head and start coming across like a Letterman monologue. If it is a newspaper that occasionally swashbuckles on its news pages, an Uncle Errol Flynn kind of paper, the rules tend to be looser on the editorial page. You can get away with a lot, and tell some truths in vivid ways.

Editorials for required occasions

But even Uncle Ned might have a few surprises in him. He might have a patriotic core that stirs when the old-fashioned flowery language soars.

For instance, I have found it useful on holidays, when the readers expect some kind of commemoration, to reach back to when the holiday really mattered, when people cared the most and the best writing was done. Memorial Day is perfect for this. It has become a bland, vague celebra-

Chapter 5
Stretching the Form

tion of patriotism, one that barely merits a parade. Right after the Civil War, though, when it was Decoration Day and involved decorating the graves of the fallen, the sacrifices of soldiers were still fresh, and the oratory reflected it. During World Wars I and II, when the very fate of democracy seemed threatened and sacrifices were being made daily, the same was true.

No rule book says you cannot appropriate a stirring oration from those eras (properly credited, of course) and run it in the paper as a commemoration of the holiday as it was long ago when it mattered most. The Internet (and the public library) have enough examples to last through a very long editorial writing career, and the readers love them at least as much as they love "Yes, Virginia" at Christmas time, an affection I personally find a little incomprehensible although I have run it in one newspaper or another on Christmas Eve for more than thirty years.

Roger Harris at the *Star-Ledger* has developed a strange specialty based in large part on his culinary loathing of turkey. Each year, he puts his strong feelings into loopy near-poetry. In 1999, he began with a Wordsworth quotation, followed by a substantial list of things for which he gives thanks. This list conspicuously did not include turkey as an entree. "Do anything you want to the turkey," he wrote, "as long as you don't roast it and bring it to the Thanksgiving table."

Come to think of it, one of the best things to remember is that there is no rule book. I have always felt fortunate that I became an editorial writer without knowing a bloody thing about edi-

torial writing. Some may say that is still the case, but it has been helpful. Although there is no rule book, there are a few things worth remembering. Violating them is no crime; it's merely inadvisable most of the time.

The basic idea that all of us ought to have tattooed on some visible appendage is that the best editorials focus on a single idea. Just one. Not two. This is not meant in a simple-minded, sound-bite kind of way. It does not mean that the entire editorial can be summed up in a brief sentence. If that is the case, just write the brief sentence. All it means is that if you do not know where you are going, no reader is going to enjoy getting there with you. If you have to ask at an editorial meeting, "What are we going to say?" it is most likely best not to say anything. People will the next day be asking one another, "What did they say?" Many an editorial subject can be discussed endlessly without ever getting to a cogent explanation of what we think about it. If I may be pretentious for a moment and quote a French intellectual, nobody has said this better than Andre Maurois: "The difficult part in an argument is not to defend one's opinion, but rather to know it."

That is exactly the point at which inventive editorials are born. Thinking and discussing exactly what we want to say determines the approach. If, for instance, we want to say that the mayor is a blockhead, it will likely require a well-mustered series of facts that lead inexorably to that conclusion (assuming, of course, that the mayor has not committed some unspeakable gaffe that makes it obvious). On the other hand, if the point is Madonna's total lack of musi-

Stretching the Form

cal talent, a quick smartass remark will probably do the job. Sometimes a mental picture comes to mind. And sometimes, nothing that hasn't been said a bazillion times before surfaces. That's when you write about something else that day.

Tragic events, for example, become no more or less tragic if the *Daily Bugle* takes a position strongly opposing tragedy. The only thing that happens if it does is that nobody reads the ensuing editorial. This kind of thing might be a job best left to the cartoonist, even though the cartoonist will no doubt complain about actually being asked to draw a cliché. The one basic reason that a good cartoon can draw infinitely more response than any editorial is its focus, its ability to take one idea and boil it down to its absolute essence, like a veal stock. A cartoon is the ultimate reduction of a good editorial. That is one of the reasons that cartoonists, however goofy, are always worth listening to. They have spent their entire working lives reducing a complicated subject to a single, bold image. The good ones are original to boot.

The editorial I think of as my personal best was short, cartoony and based on a single idea. A dictator was dead and we were glad. The headline was "Adios, Dictator." The entire text was: "They say only the good die young. Generalissimo Francisco Franco was 82. Seems about right." Even then, purifying and reducing an idea is worthwhile. In retrospect, that "Seems about right" looks unnecessary. The editorial had not been simplified all the way.

Just as every editorial, no matter how routine or how bold, must be based on one idea, every trick you pull out has to be in the service of that idea. The *Philadelphia Daily News* did a marvelous stunt on a editorial about the Food and Drug Administration requiring larger print on prescription bottles. Aware of the aging of the Baby Boomers, as anyone not living in a cave in the Canadian Rockies must be by now, the newspaper gradually reduced the type size as the editorial continued, emphasizing the point it was making with those shrinking words.

Every trick is at your disposal. Should the local slumlord die, nothing prevents you from running a photograph of one of his especially terrible properties, along with a simple line such as: "Joe Slumlord 1927–2000: His Legacy." Obituary editorials, oddly enough, lend themselves to that kind of brief treatment, in the shortest possible editorial. When Grateful Dead bandleader Jerry Garcia died, *The Post-Standard* of Syracuse ran a single, perfect word: "Bummer."

One goal on occasion is to slap the readers awake with a simple concept that clarifies a point or brings one up. A columnist I know got mail from everywhere complaining about a very simple perception. It was his theory that George W. Bush went to Yale, a place full of great thinkers, and chose to drink and party, then went to Texas, home of great drinkers and partiers, and chose to begin thinking. He saw a magnificent cognitive dissonance. But he also made a point that resonated, favorably or not, with a lot of readers. Whatever else they did, they reacted. Woody Allen famously remarked that most of life is showing

Stretching the Form

up; for editorial writers, the secret is often getting noticed at all.

Here is where Uncles Ned and Errol return. We are writing for newspapers that people know as well as their own families. When I was in Philadelphia, it wasn't hard to discern the totally different personalities of the *Inquirer,* the *Evening Bulletin* and the *Daily News.* Each one had a distinct voice. You could get away with murder at the *Daily News.* The *Bulletin* was serious and respectable and the *Inquirer* was crusading, influential and just a tad full of itself. Different voices required a different writing approach.

In addition to the difficulty of writing humor in the first place, we have to worry about the right tone of voice. Elegant sallies work in one place, jokes that seem to have an accompanying drum roll in another. What works beautifully in *The Charlotte Observer* may not work at all in the *New York Post.*

Think you're funny?

Let's assume that you are fully aware of your newspaper's personality, and that you haven't reduced a publisher to insane rage in a long time. That doesn't mean humor is automatically mastered. I used to write a column that was a variation on the late Jimmy Cannon's "Nobody Asked Me, But" columns, a series of one-liners running to full column length. I have never worked so hard before or since. Each line had to pop like stand-up comedy. It could take as long to write a single item as it would to write a complicated budget editorial. Comedy isn't funny business.

Comedy also leaves you open to that most devastating of responses: "I don't get it." Never mind that someone, usually someone who outranks you, has just acknowledged total inability to comprehend. They do not mind a bit; in fact, a surprising number of people take pride in "not getting it." The fact is that there will always be someone who does not get it. And some who do get it won't like it. A politician who can withstand daily hammering with blunt instruments will frequently go ballistic when he discerns that he's being made fun of. His supporters will be worse. That's when you know you have made your point.

Writing to get a laugh is both dangerous and difficult. The only surefire test is the one every stand-up comic knows: You take it out in front of an audience and see what happens. Read their reaction. They will always tell you how funny you are—or aren't.

Remember that the secret of all comedy is timing. "I'm thinking" is not particularly funny. But set it up with a stickup man demanding of Jack Benny, "Your money or your life," followed by a thirty-second pause, and it is hilarious. Just as serious writing is dependent on tone and timing, "writing funny" absolutely demands it. You can ruin a magnificent punch line by not setting it up deliberately, step by step. You can ruin everybody's day by actually announcing up front that what you are about to do is funny. Just think of the drunk at the last party who prefaced a joke with, "This one will kill you." Generally, all it does is make you wish one of you had died.

Never forget that humor can be the most effective way of making a serious point. It is one thing to counter an argument point-by-point. It is quite another to demolish an opponent with a single line. For instance, if you quickly read the transcript of the 1984 debate between Ronald Reagan and Walter Mondale, you might come to the conclusion that Mondale won. But Mondale himself acknowledges that the debate—and the election itself—were decided when Reagan eliminated the issue of his own advanced age with the line, "I am not going to exploit for political purposes my opponent's youth and inexperience." Even the mortally wounded Mondale laughed.

The *Fort Worth Star-Telegram*, confronted by a legislator who routinely killed legislation with parliamentary maneuvers that kept bills from even being considered, used a wonderful technique. It portrayed her, complete with fangs, in a horror movie poster, "I Know What You Did Last Session," complete with critics' blurbs and tease lines. It was brutally effective, although this is as good a place as any to point out that any technique has limitations. Overuse will destroy the effectiveness of anything. You wouldn't want to run a movie poster every week.

Typography often is helpful. *The Arizona Republic*, facing in 1988 the end of the game for Arizona's unspeakable governor, wrote the following paragraph and floated it in a sea of white space that normally would be occupied by a full editorial:

Indicted. Booked. Fingerprinted. Arraigned. Evan Mecham— governor, chief of state government, holder of the highest elected office in the state of Arizona—facing trial by criminal court and impeachment, must, within four days, choose resignation or recall. It is time to end the agony in Arizona. It is time for courage and sacrifice and wisdom. Evan Mecham, the moment of resignation has truly come.

Here's another editorial that makes good use of white space, a 1992 piece by Guy MacMillin of *The Keene Sentinel* in New Hampshire:

A Dry Brow

We thought about publishing an editorial today concerning Japanese Prime Minister Kiichi Miyazawa's outrageous remark that Americans "lack a work ethic . . . to live by the sweat of their brow." But we decided to knock off early and watch a little TV.

What followed was a great deal of white space.

The point often is to stay off the beat, to come at readers from an unexpected direction, even if you're denouncing or praising the same old stuff. If you pick out an aspect of an issue that is unique, one that illuminates from the underside, that shows how a carefully built issue is dependent on lousy assumptions, what you get is the written equivalent of jazz. Keep playing the same way everytime, and you've got the ricky-tick sound of Kay Kyser's Kollege of Musical Knowledge. Frequently, this kind of editorial questions why today's big issue is an issue at all, whether it is symbolic or even irrele-

Stretching the Form

vant. Newspapers wrote endlessly in 1960 about the Chinese threat to the Formosan islands of Quemoy and Matsu, for example. It would have been more illuminating to write about how the debate itself was showing a shift in American attitudes toward Taiwan and China rather than the simpler and easier call to arms.

Sometimes the grin of recognition is as good as a belly laugh. Absolutely straight presentation of an absurd premise can slowly build into hilarity that devastates the premise. Try to keep a straight face, for example, while reading the tax plan of either major party candidate in the 2000 election. All an editorial writer would have to do is reduce all the verbiage, then pile one ridiculous assumption atop another until the whole *furshlugginer* mess collapses. Punch line is optional. If you did it right, they're already laughing.

Know what you're good at. Writing an irony-laced essay is different from writing one-liners that demand rim shot punctuation. Television has taken several generations of humorists and tried to ram them into one-minute segments. It never works. A Texas humorist, like the splendid Molly Ivins of the *Fort Worth Star-Telegram*, needs time to set up atmosphere, character and tone. Her immortal description of the Texas House speaker—"If he gets any dumber, we'll have to water him twice a day"—is funniest with a calm, laconic introduction.

Remember that little is more painful than humor that doesn't work. Especially satire. Especially satire in an era in which everything you hear sounds as if it were already

satire and comes prelaced with irony. Always bear in mind the old show business axiom that satire closes on Saturday night. The odds against comprehension are high. Approach with care and more than a little fear.

One-liners are easier to put across, so if you have a gift for one-liners, save them up. Wait for the right occasion. Carry with you the humble realization that most Americans get their political news from the late-night talk show monologues, written by professional comedy writers and delivered impeccably. Also carry with you the confidence that a good one is more effective than a dozen standard editorials. Don't waste your best material for something that doesn't quite fit. Do not, under any circumstances, try to inflate a one-liner to more than it is. Be happy with it. And if you write something you think is hilarious and show it to five people who don't laugh, be merciless. Comedy is serious business. Kill it.

Anything might work. Anything. I personally despise poetry in the newspaper, in large part because it encourages readers to send in execrable doggerel. But I have to admit this 1992 *Arizona Republic* editorial by Mark Genrich works perfectly:

Whose woods these are we think we know.

His office is in ADOT though;
William Belt, the bureaucrat
Has said the woods are full of snow.

Our little car must think it queer
To stop and see a chain saw near

Chapter 5
Stretching the Form

Between the woods and frozen lake
The darkest evening of the year.

The Flagstaff route is lined with wood;
Where tall pine trees and others stood.
It matters not about those trees,
ADOT wants them gone for good.

The woods are lovely, dark and deep,
But he has promises to keep,
And trees to kill before he sleeps,
A thousand trees before he sleeps.

In end, the secrets are simple and the rules are few. If you have something to say, spit it out. If you don't, shut up. The rest is mere technique.

Chapter 6

The Forum Function

By Ronald D. Clark

By now, after five chapters paying homage to editorials, the editors and preceding authors have firmly established the principal theme of this book. That is, the highest and best use of your time is to tell readers or viewers what your newspaper or TV station thinks about the important issues of the day.

Let me offer an alternate view. Without trying to puncture the significance of editorials, I want to make the case for paying at least as much attention, if not more, to the forum function of newspapers and television. In the first instance, we speak and our audience reads or listens. In the second, our audience speaks.

Don't treat the forum function as an afterthought. Sure, part of our duty is to exercise our intellectual ability. But who says we must act as if our thoughts are routinely superior to others? Shouldn't we define our role—at least in part—as widening the circle and bringing many others with valid opinions onto our pages and into the conversation?

This often runs counter to what we editorialists were taught, and cer-

About the author

Ronald D. Clark

Ronald D. Clark is editorial page editor of the *Pioneer Press* in St. Paul, Minnesota, a position he has held since 1981. His priorities have included expanding local access to the opinion pages, and being more selective about writing editorials while exploring other options for leading community debate and discussion. Previously, he held various reporting, editing and editorial page positions at *The Beacon Journal* in Akron, Ohio, where he was part of a team that won a Pulitzer Prize for coverage of the Kent State University shootings in 1970.

Chapter 6
The Forum Function

tainly to tradition. Our training emphasized the history of editorials, the great editorialists who went before us and the research and writing of powerful and effective opinions. Our systems of rewards and recognition put the highest premium on what comes out of our minds, not on the breadth of community participation and interaction that we promote or generate.

No prizes honor expanding letters to the editor, forming community advisory boards or boards of contributors, convening forums on sensitive and difficult issues that divide the community. But if our audiences, not our peers, controlled the prizes, things might be different.

I don't mean to suggest a choice between one or the other—between leading with our voice and leading with our ability to create a forum. Obviously, we do both. But if we see ourselves more as editorial writers than as stewards of a moderated forum, if our self-esteem comes only from the opinions we create rather than the opinions we allow others to present, then we risk being marginalized.

"Today's editorial page editor is challenged by an era that offers audiences a variety of media that reach out in increasingly personal ways as various as the Internet and Oprah," says syndicated columnist Clarence Page of the *Chicago Tribune.* "As we move into the new century, I think editorial pages should expand the

---

The game has changed

The objective of the editorial game has changed. Before, the reader supported and respected the well-formulated, eloquent, one-sided debate of an issue. It was as if reading the position of the editorialist helped secure or justify the reader in his own beliefs. Presenting the masterful, moral position that reflects the sensibility of primarily one segment of society has given way to the need for a more open forum, hosting a wide variety of perspectives and voices.

—*Jamie Baker, student, University of Memphis*

(*The Masthead*, Fall 1999)

---

space they devote to letters and other forms of reader feedback to increase the personal relationship our audiences have with us. We need more than ever to send a message that they are a part of what we do, not just a big monolithic public to be lectured to."

"My ideal editorial page is a newspaper counterpart to a lively dinner conversation," says Nancy Q. Keefe, a retired editorial page columnist from White Plains, New York. "Invite a comfortable number of people so that everyone has a chance to talk and listen. They shouldn't be all alike at any one time or over time. Through a year of dinners, you'd want women and men, young and old, gay and straight, of many colors, faiths and national origins. You'd want people who are highly educated and self-taught, readers and TV viewers, capitalists and socialists from the mainstream and fringe of every neighborhood in town. Everybody contributes to the conversation, and can say thoughtful or outrageous things. The only hard and fast rule is we all have to be civil to one another."

Just one more thought on this point. For all the veneration we give to editorials, few of us are ever really pleased with the quality of our own work. Seldom do we think we have enough time to research and write editorials, or for that matter to find good topics that aren't too complex.

Chapter 6
The Forum Function

University of Georgia journalism professor Ernest C. Hynds, in research in 1994, found that four-fifths of editorial writers responding to a survey said that a lack of time for research and writing editorials was a problem, and about half said it was a "major" problem. More than half also cited finding good subjects and dealing with the complexity of issues as problems, said Hynds.

So would someone please explain why so many in our profession resist any infringement on either the number of editorials we write or the primacy we attach to their importance? If we editors and writers acknowledge that our editorials often are less than our best work, what makes us think that our readers and viewers don't see the same shortcomings? Or that at least some of our readers might not have just as much worth saying—or more—on a variety of topics as we do?

What are the elements of an engaging and lively forum function? And what are some innovations in use or under development around the country?

Consider letters as a barometer of how well your newspaper or station is engaging readers or viewers. The more you receive, the more you're connecting. The fewer you receive, the stronger the sign that you're putting the masses to sleep.

Getting them in the door

By now, everyone knows the importance of accepting letters by e-mail and fax, not just snail mail. Where there is disagreement is over whether to take phone-in letters.

The *Tallahassee Democrat*, for example, welcomes anonymous messages on voice mail, then transcribes and prints them. "Zing," as the feature is known, is very popular, attracting seventy-five percent of the *Democrat's* readers, says Mary Ann Lindley, editorial page editor. "I'd argue that the anonymous call-in line— on which we receive very brief and to-the-point comments, not long letters—offers a way to vent frustrations in a government town where people have indeed been fired over letters to the editor, and who often feel intimidated about commenting for fear of losing their jobs." "Zing" also appeals to the sound-bite generation and the online community, she adds.

Such arguments don't persuade Charles Reinken,

By the numbers

Research in 1994 on letters to the editor found that:

• 23 percent of responding papers publish fewer than half of letters received; 77 percent publish more than half received.

• 40.5 percent of all papers limit letter length to 251 to 500 words; 15.5 percent have no word limit; 35.1 percent limit letters to 250 words or fewer.

• Anonymous letters are very likely to be rejected 93.9 percent of the time.

• 59.9 percent of respondents said unfair personal attacks are a basis for rejecting letters.

• 36.2 percent of all papers have no limit on how often they will publish letters from a particular source; 4.7 percent limit publication to once a week; 37.2 percent limit writers to once a month.

• 3.4 percent of papers will withhold a writer's name by request; 10.8 percent will withhold it for good cause.

• About 90 percent of larger papers (100,001 to 500,000-plus circulation) shorten letters, while only 49.4 percent of smaller (25,000 circulation or less) papers do.

Source: Suraj Kapoor, associate professor, communication department, Illinois State University

(*The Masthead,* Summer 1995)

The Forum Function

deputy editorial page editor of the *Omaha World-Herald.* "What do you do about verification?" he asks. "If you don't have some system, however imperfect, for checking authorship, you have either been conned or are waiting to be.... Any time we miss the opportunity to exercise what little custodianship we have over writing and rational thought, the linguistic infidels inch that much closer."

The *Belleville News-Democrat* in Illinois allows writers to voice their opinions anonymously one day a week. Lori Browning, editorial page editor, explains, "This is a way to give a voice to lots of people who otherwise would not write letters to the editor." The newspaper uses about half the anonymous submissions it receives. "Anything we think is libelous, or that contains statements we can't verify as facts, we dump," Browning adds. The feature is very popular, although some readers still tell the newspaper that it should publish no letters without the authors' names.

My advice: People tend to be more responsible and want to stay close to the facts when their names are attached to their writing. Anonymity gives people license to be irresponsible.

Selecting

Most of us publish more than half the letters we receive, but some of us are required, because of space constraints, to be more selective. How do you make decisions about what stays and what goes? Here are some considerations:

• Ask yourself what is of interest to your readers. Be alert to the subjects that draw clusters of letters, taking

conflicting points of view.

• Have a bias for the critics of the newspaper and its content rather than for the fans. There is a direct correlation between your credibility and your willingness to have your views criticized in print.

• Think about diversity of views— by age, race, gender, political orientation, place of residence (city, suburb, exurb, rural). Don't give readers an excuse for concluding that the newspaper or TV station doesn't have room for people who look, act and think like they do.

• Evaluate whether certain popular topics have run their course. At the same time, however, appreciate that often the public is just getting warmed up to a subject at the point we're getting bored with it.

• Toss the letters from outside your circulation or viewing area unless there is a compelling reason to use them and they are tied to content in your paper or on your station.

• Check for libel, factual errors, tone.

• Be open to requests to withhold the name of a writer if the message is important and publication might bring the writer physical or economic harm, unwarranted humiliation or harassment or other devastating consequences.

• Consider whether you want to limit the frequency with which individual letter writers can get their views published or on the air. Some do, using it to assure access to the widest audience; others don't, judging each letter on its merit.

• Decide whether you want to publish poetry (most larger papers

Chapter 6

The Forum Function

don't) or give space to those advocating for a particular religious faith (again, most larger papers don't).

Editing

Of course you should remove or correct obvious factual errors and take out potentially libelous statements. But don't assume your job is done at that point. If you show a little neglect in some of the following areas, be prepared for an angry phone call or visit.

• Avoid the temptation to rewrite letters beyond minor changes. Oh, it's fine to shift around paragraphs or sentences, or make other changes that make the message more effective. But if what you publish is different in tone, style and vocabulary from what you received, you risk emasculating the writer's voice. Aggressive editing of this sort has sent at least one letter writer to the Minnesota News Council in my state, seeking to have the newspaper scolded. The council agreed with the letter writer. A better approach is to send the letter back to the writer for changes or stick it in the round file. At the same time, don't hold letter writers to the same standards you expect from journalists and other professionals. Cut them a little slack.

• Be sensitive to concerns about balance, especially on controversial topics. One way is to collect letters on the same subject over several days

---

In a Pig's Eye

The News-Sentinel in Fort Wayne, Indiana, distributes a forty-two-page booklet to its readers titled "In a Pig's Eye: How to argue with the editorial page." It contains tips on writing letters and guest columns, as well as tips on logic, punctuation, spelling, research and structure. For more information, contact Leo Morris, editorial page editor. E-mail: lmorris@news-sentinel.com

---

before making your selections, thus increasing your chances of having a variety of views from which to choose. If you randomly run letters on one side one day and those with opposite views on another day, you risk being perceived as unfair by those who aren't everyday readers. Don't fall into the trap of running an equal proportion of letters from various perspectives on hot topics. Balance doesn't mean exact quotas. We're not giving readers the results of a scientific poll.

• Understand that you will be subject to organized campaigns to flood you with letters from one perspective on a hot topic. This is all the more reason not to feel obliged to run exact quotas.

• There are frauds and phonies out there who want their opinions to appear but not their names. For example, in the middle of a labor dispute, my newspaper once received a letter signed with the name of a hospital executive. We later determined the letter actually was written by a union member. Not good. To sniff out the mischief makers, many newspapers call every writer and verify authenticity before publication. Others use their instincts to verify only those that look suspicious. There's no single rule for all situations, except err on the side of caution.

What if you spot a factual error in a letter? You have several options. If

The Forum Function

Online: The New Frontier

Marrying "dead-tree journalism" and the Internet is where newspapers (and presumably TV stations) should be going in the future to reverse many of the complaints writers now have about the handling of their letters. So says Steve Outing, who provides news and analysis for Editor & Publisher Interactive about the online news industry. In a column December 22, 1999, he suggested ways that newspapers can make their letter writers happier and also demonstrate their support for the free exchange of ideas. To overcome the lack of physical space for letters in the newspaper, he offers these solutions:

• The letters page editor combs through the regular onslaught of reader mail and selects the best ones for publication in the print edition.

• The editor weeds out the junk—the letters written by demented souls and the ones that make no sense; the letters that are thinly disguised commercial messages; the "me too" letters that make no new points; the letters that contain profanity or are libelous; etc.

• That leaves a pile of letters from rational, intelligent people who didn't make the "best" pile for the print edition, but deserve to seen by your publication's readers. Publish those on your Web site in a "Letters to the Editor Plus" area.

• In your print edition, include contextual links to the online letters to the editor (especially those on the same topic).

• For each and every letter published online, allow online readers to click and fill out a form to post a follow-up note to the original letter. Each letter then has the potential to spawn its own discussion thread. (Also consider grouping letters on specific topics. Allow a Web user to search for all letters on teen violence, for example, and turn up not only the published letters—online and in print—but also the user follow-up comments to the letters.

it's an obvious error around which the letter is built, you shouldn't use the letter. You could notify the writer of the error and ask if he wants to correct it. Minor errors—incorrect dates, misspelled names and other mistakes that are secondary to the writer's main point—can be corrected by the editor without consulting the writer.

One caution, though. Resist the tendency to label as a factual error what in truth is a matter of opinion or judgment. Also, if you adhere to a strict policy of eliminating all factual errors in letters, you could be spending much more time fact-checking than the demands on you might allow.

Other judgment calls

There is no end to questions that come up about letters to the editor. Here are a few more that you'll encounter at some point, if you haven't already.

Q: Should employees of the newspaper or TV station, in any capacity, be able to write letters for publication or broadcast?

A: Those media that prohibit the use of employee letters usually do so with the idea of preserving the sanctity of the letters space for readers or viewers. Using employee letters would harm credibility, they contend, and raise concerns about an unfair advantage for insiders. Enforcement is not always uniform, however, especially with larger companies, where it is more difficult for the letters editor to know all employees. Some newspapers cut slack for family members of employees, however, on the theory that the ban shouldn't extend outside company walls. Others, though, give no such amnesty to family members, on the theory that it would be just as difficult to explain publication of a letter by the advertising director's spouse, for instance, as the advertising director.

Q: Should you first seek permission before putting out a letter writer's e-mail address?

A: The policy of D. Michael Heywood, editorial page editor of *The Columbian* in Vancouver,

The Forum Function

Washington, is typical. "When we first started publishing letters received by e-mail, we published the e-mail address as part of the signature," Heywood notes. "Readers and correspondents didn't like that, in part considering it an unwarranted variation from our usual policy of publishing only the name and town. We gave it up after just a couple of weeks. . . . Now, upon a correspondent's request for reader response, we will include the e-mail address in the body of the letter." Subjecting letter writers to hate mail and harassment are the big concerns, the same reason most media don't give out or publish phone numbers or home addresses of letter writers.

Q: Is it ever OK to fabricate a letter?

A: No. In fact, an editorial page editor in Utica, New York, was fired after admitting he had made up eleven published letters.

Q: Should you run racist letters or other hate-filled speech?

A: The question provokes a range of response, judging from an exchange that took place on NCEW's online mailing list.

"Printing contrarian—even offensive— views is one of the roles I cherish," wrote John H. Taylor Jr., editorial page editor of *The News Journal* in Wilmington, Delaware. "It reminds people that hate-driven folks are out there." Added Jeffrey M. Brody, opinion page editor of *The Sun* in Bremerton, Washington, "It's not up to me to edit opinions. Force the vicious and ridiculous opinions to survive in the marketplace of ideas; don't pretend to your readers that they don't exist." A different perspective came from Gale Hammons, associate editor of *The Modesto Bee* in California. "We do not serve our readers well by publishing the dumb letter and its progeny."

At my paper we shy away from running racist letters, but each newspaper has to arrive at its own policy after examining local values, needs and expectations.

Recognition

For all the challenges that letters pose, for all the headaches they create, for all the time they eat up in selection and editing, they're still a bargain. What other source of content do we have that flows so steadily into our newspapers or TV stations, draws so much attention and readership or viewer interest— for free? If you recognize the value created by the mail, then consider showing it.

Newspapers celebrate letter writers in a variety of ways: presenting Silver Pen awards annually to writers of the ten most impressive letters and taking them to lunch or dinner; presenting an ID card to the best letter writers and giving them total access to the newspaper, including news and editorial meetings, for a year; holding workshops for letter writers.

Instant response

Start building an e-mail list of your letter writers and correspondents. Then, whip out that list when you need reader feedback on an idea you're thinking about implementing, or when you need a quick turnaround of letters on a major breaking news story. You can build general purpose lists and specialty lists based on various demographic areas and interests.

Chapter 6
The Forum Function

My newspaper picks one outstanding letter a month and invites the writers and their guests to a semi-annual breakfast with the editorial page staff and publisher or senior newsroom executives. Then we reprint the letters.

If you have a role in deciding what columns make it onto your opinion pages, let me repeat an earlier admonition: Don't assume that responsibility is secondary to the opportunity to write thundering editorials.

Consider the parallels with baseball, especially with the teams that have had player/managers. The player/manager not only took his turn at bat and in the field, but also was responsible for the final score and all other aspects of the club's on-field performance. In the same way, opinion pages need a variety of skills and abilities in those invited to play on the newspaper's team. As the manager, you are responsible for putting together a lineup that will score runs, cover all the positions, hit for singles and for power, swing from the right and the left, excite fans and give them their money's worth.

Variety

More than opinions, columnists are a tool for bringing color, breadth, diversity, texture, personality, controversy, humor, pathos, fine writing and enlightenment to our pages. A veteran newspaper reporter and columnist at *The Beacon Journal* once told me there are two points to consider in selecting a columnist: (1.) Can the person write? and (2.) Does the person have anything worth saying? Beyond that simple test, however, there are many more considerations in selecting a stable of columnists and many ways of using them.

Remember the dinner parties that Nancy Q. Keefe wanted to host? Think about the guests you want to see around the table on your pages, about the voices you want to hear in conversation.

Finding columnists

The challenge most of us face is not in finding acceptable syndicated or wire columnists (syndicate salespersons and the wire services bring them to our door) or staff columnists (we inherit them or have ready access to those we might want to bring aboard). Rather, it is in discovering capable and provocative local talent. Here is how some newspapers and TV stations do it:

• Stage a contest. Kay Semion did that at the *Dayton Daily News*. In 1999, she wrote a column asking

---

Making changes

Is it OK to make extensive changes in a manuscript from a guest columnist and proceed to publication without first reviewing the alterations with the writer? No, said Rich Bard, writing as the Sunday opinion editor of *The Miami Herald* in the Spring 1993 issue of *The Masthead*. He advised:

"I know editors who do extensive editing and cutting without consulting the authors before publication. But I have made it a practice to let each author review his or her work if it has been edited heavily or extensively. (Of course, I retain final control over content, but I don't want to publish unless the author is satisfied.) . . . I do this first as a courtesy; after all, the article has the author's name on it, not mine. And I'm well aware that editing can unintentionally obfuscate as well as clarify meaning. In any case, it saves me unneeded headaches on Monday morning and promotes good will."

readers to send in two 650-word sample columns, a photo, some background information and three ideas for future columns. She wanted to select ten readers to write twice a month for a year about local issues, for a token per-column payment (twenty-five dollars). More than one hundred sixty readers sent in samples. Her choices included a talented high-school sophomore, a former psychiatric nurse, an urban planner, a divorce lawyer and a farm wife.

The State in Columbia, South Carolina, also took applications, received three hundred twenty-one, selected eight and prints two a week. *The Star* in Kansas City recruits and selects a stable of community writers to do one piece a month. We in St. Paul run one community column a week from a designated group, but also two or three others from among those submitted on spec. When we launched our Community Columnists program in 1999, we received seven hundred thirty-four applications—an encouraging sign of interest, though overwhelming. We chose seven, and put them on a rotating schedule that netted seven columns from each over the year. Our second invitation drew responses from about two hundred applicants, a much more manageable number.

• Identify prospects and go after them. David DuBuisson, former editorial page editor of the *News & Record* in Greensboro, North Carolina, says he and his staff "placed particular emphasis on people who were different from the usual run of local contributors. We looked for women, minorities and young people, though not to the exclusion of middle-aged white guys." They came up with sixty names, invited thirty to apply, hoping to get twenty-five. They did, but quickly discovered that not all had the requisite writing skills, ability to meet deadlines or broad interests. They subsequently modified their process to include tryouts, wherein prospects were invited to submit one-shot op-eds to determine if they could write and deliver on time. "It saved a lot of time and headaches. But of course the yield of columns was reduced proportionately," DuBuisson adds. (Under new management, however, the paper dropped the program.)

• Work with the news bureau or media relations office of the college or university in your town or ones nearby. Many of them maintain lists of facul-

Editorial writer as columnist

When an editorial writer also produces regular columns for the opinion pages, what conflicts and issues are likely to arise? Here are a few.

• Should the columnist be permitted to state a different position than the editorial board on a topic already addressed by the board? In my newspaper, each editorial writer also produces columns. Disagreement with the newspaper's editorial policy in a signed column is acceptable as a means of promoting lively and healthy debate. However, at *The Miami Herald*, editor Jim Hampton wrote in the Winter 1997 *Masthead*, neither the publisher nor the editor nor editorial writers may contradict editorial policy, since it would confuse readers and dilute the institution's views.

• Should an editorial writer/columnist be permitted to advocate for or against certain political candidates after the newspaper has made its endorsements in those races? My newspaper takes the position that individual editorial board members can write columns about various political races before endorsements, but not afterward in a way that appears to be a personal endorsement.

• Should columnists be able to write about topics, activities or organizations in which they are directly involved? This requires careful thought. It is one thing to use knowledge gained through volunteer work such as helping first-graders develop their reading skills, or serving meals in a homeless shelter. It is another to write in such a way as to gain an advantage for the writer's agency over another, or to write on behalf of an organization that is compensating the columnist or to act as an unofficial (or official) publicity chair.

ty with expertise and a willingness to comment on various subjects. But don't assume that because they have fancy degrees, they can write for a mass audience and not be boring.

• Work with high school or college journalism faculty to identify promising younger writers and encourage submissions from them.

• Develop a database of names, e-mail addresses, phone numbers and areas of expertise or interest of those you see submitting eye-catching letters to the editor or guest columns. Try asking them for a guest column on the right topic at the right time.

• Create a community advisory board, selecting representatives who bring knowledge, history, culture, life experiences and perspectives that may be missing from the editorial board. Ask the advisory board members to write occasional columns.

What doesn't work? Editorial page editors point to some of their failures:

• Making a general request in print for readers to comment on a specific issue.

• Speaking to civic groups and clubs and encouraging members to submit columns. Editors in Fort Wayne, Indiana, and Detroit are among those who have tried it, without much to show for their time and effort. However, Spokane, Washington, has

Connecting readers and columnists

Readers like to connect with columnists and give them feedback. Editorial pages that care about their readers should make that easy. If you're not regularly helping readers reach columnists now, consider doing so. The easiest and most common way? List contact information for each columnist. This could be an e-mail or snail mail address, or telephone number. Make this a condition of getting a piece published in the paper and you won't have any trouble. However, be sure you're providing some form of contact information for yourselves before asking others to do the same.

reached a different conclusion. Three editorial writers at *The Spokesman-Review* carry the title of interactive editor. Besides writing one editorial a week, they also are responsible for being visible in the community, attending meetings, volunteering on civic committees, speaking about the newspaper, recruiting guest columnists and helping them organize and polish their writing. These interactive editors also have organized and led community forums on issues. "I really am interested in the business of finding articles written by people who actually know what they are writing about," says John Webster, editorial page editor of *The Spokesman-Review*. "We are such generalists, even though we do develop areas of expertise. To get a column by someone with real expertise, and print that—there is value to that, too."

Using columnists

This is a place for creativity. Your obligation is to the readers more than the writers. It is relatively easy to consider each column as an individual, stand-alone element of your pages, where your responsibility is to edit with a light pencil, write a catchy headline and strip it across the page with a head shot of the writer. But consider some options:

Chapter 6
The Forum Function

• Pro/con or point/counterpoint. Our readers in the Twin Cities consistently tell us how much they appreciate this format. They have a sense that the newspaper is attempting to be fair in presenting opinion. You can do this with two staff columns on the same topic, two guest columns or two syndicated writers. Or you can mix and match: a staff column and a guest writer, a guest writer and a syndicated columnist. Just be careful not to needlessly give the appearance of stacking the deck one way or the other, either with length, display, use of art or graphics or similar techniques. And consider whether it's unfair to allow one writer to see and react to the manuscript of the second, while denying the second the same advantage. The fairest way is to give each writer a topic and length, and disclose that this will be part of a package presenting two contrasting views on the issue.

• Roundup. On a hot issue, consider using a roundup of comments from a number of writers in the same space that you might normally devote to one or two. If you find ten national columnists, including some of your syndicated purchases, addressing a singular national or international event—a massacre at a school, for instance—why not lift out the essential points or conclusions of a half dozen and package them to give readers a flavor of the diversity of opinion on the subject?

• Forum. Consider asking several individuals in your community to address an important topic and give them a length limit. We did this recently in response to a *Newsweek* cover story suggesting that blacks collectively have never before achieved such a large piece of the American dream. We asked a half-dozen black residents of the Twin Cities whether they agreed; the variety of responses we got back was more impressive than if we had just given space to one person.

Chapter 7

Layout and Presentation

By Laird B. Anderson

Pat McCubbin, associate editor of the editorial pages at *The Plain Dealer* in Cleveland, every morning stares at a blank editorial page and op-ed page and thinks of the exquisite challenge that lies ahead: how she and her colleagues can blend design and the written word in the best way to grab readers. During the week, she also is contemplating the five-page Sunday Forum section in terms of melding story presentation, illustrations, photos, color and graphics to enhance the commentary.

McCubbin and her associates are in the midst of presentation experiments. They're looking, said graphics director Ken Marshall, for "visual surprises" to help drive home the point of view. The editorial cartoon, for instance, is now printed in color on Sunday.

The newspaper's "Forum Of Opinion & Ideas" page on Saturday has replaced the traditional op-ed page. It offers a new idea called "The Pulse" (Figure 1), a look at opinion polls using charts, graphs and illustrations published in color and designed by Marshall. Another new and evolving Sunday page, also using color, anchors an "Inside Politics" column with columns called "Eye on the world" and "Ad watch" which evaluates TV campaign ads, along with a "How they voted" look at how Ohio's United States representatives and senators voted during the week.

The newspaper is considering

About the author
Laird B. Anderson

Laird B. Anderson is a retired professor of journalism. He taught opinion writing at American University for over twenty years. A former reporter for *The Wall Street Journal* in Chicago and Washington, he is co-editor of *Pulitzer Prize Editorials: America's Best Editorial Writing, 1917–1993*.

Layout and Presentation

once or twice a week replacing the op-ed page with a full page of letters. These would be enhanced by illustrations and occasionally pictures highlighting writers "with a special voice or cause to make the pages more personal and reader-conscious," McCubbin said.

Many newspapers are making their pages more appealing to help reverse circulation declines in this era of the visual explosion. But American newspapers are playing catch-up with the foreign press. David Gray, executive director of the Society for News Design (www.snd.org) wrote in an American Society of Newspaper Editors publication, "It used to be that the rest of the world looked to the United States for leadership in design, production and innovation in newspapers. If the results of SND's annual 'Best of Newspaper Design' contest is any bellwether, then that leadership position may have been displaced in the past few years by newspapers from Spain, Central and South America, Scandinavia and the German-speaking countries." In 1999, one thousand fifty-five awards were given from a selection of thirteen thousand entries from one hundred sixty-three newspapers in twenty-one countries.

Figure 1

Figure 2

Chapter 7
Layout and Presentation

Innovation in the design of American opinion pages has come slowly, compared to the change in news sections. Still, the wind of change is ruffling the staid and traditional approach to presentation and has produced some dramatic adjustments.

At the *Austin American-Statesman* the editorial page labeled "Commentary" offers a variety of formats daily, sometimes replacing editorials with a Q&A, a signed editorial notebook, or an occasional "thank you" photo/editorial tribute. On Sunday, a single topic may get spotlighted (Figure 2). In this case the

"Who's working on the issue" section lists names and phone numbers, including then-Governor George W. Bush. Maria Henson, the Pulitzer Prize-winning deputy editorial page editor, says the mix of editorial formats is an effective element of surprise for readers.

Many editorial page editors are looking for fresh ways to spur readership. *The Pioneer Press* in Saint Paul, Minnesota, lived up to the spirit of its name on New Year's Eve in 1995. In a full-page spread, editorial page editor Ronald D. Clark announced "A New Look, Greater Depth" and illustrated the approach with three mini-pages.

Figure 3

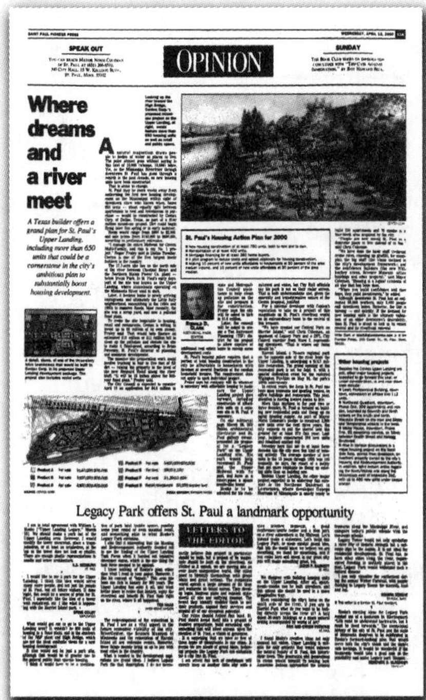

Layout and Presentation

Figure 4 -5

Starting with an example of a traditional page, he followed with two other examples that highlighted coming attractions. "In the future, we'll run fewer editorials and devote more space to other forms of opinion, such as in-depth bylined reports and point/counterpoint analysis, with greater emphasis on graphics," he said.

For example, using color, a Clark essay and letters, the newspaper published an op-ed look at a proposed project that could be a "cornerstone in the city's ambitious plan to substantially boost housing development" (Figure 3). This example became op-ed only because he could get color for this page and not the other that day, Clark said. Other innovations have included a full editorial page devoted to guest commentators discussing local public school funding. Another editorial page, as a prelude to Canada's Remembrance Day, used a guest writer's brief review of the book *Requiem,* bolstered by photos and a signed editorial writer's tribute to the one hundred thirty-five photojournalists who died in Vietnam and Indochina. Public reaction has been good, Clark said.

Among other creative and unusual initiatives:

• *The Arizona Republic,* under editorial page editor Keven Ann Willey, in 1999 ran a series of editorials mak-

Figure 6

Figure 7

ing the case for better-funded and supervised child-care facilities. Part two was a double-page spread (Figures 4 and 5). Another unusual presentation was a simple two-page listing with a brief editorial and some art of more than three thousand young Arizonans who died in World Wars I and II, Korea, Vietnam and Desert Storm, a project that took a year to develop, since no such accounting existed.

• *The Hartford Courant* ran a four-part series of editorials by Daryl Perch that aimed to demystify mental illness and promote reform of [Connecticut's] inadequate system of care. The series (Figure 6 is the final

part) was a first, said David Fink, associate editor. But in his view, editorial pages aren't staffed to experiment, with most set up habitually to use the traditional template. He argues for unpredictable presentations, but said that many will shy away because they would have to change their entire editorial page operation to accomplish them.

• *The Spokesman-Review* of Spokane, Washington, under opinion editor John D. Webster offered another example of a single-issue presentation, this one timed to coincide with an in-depth reporting project by the newsroom. The paper ran full pages detailing accidents on "The Highway

Layout and Presentation

of Heartache" and putting names and faces to the thirty-five people who died on the road in 1999 (Figure 7). A signed editorial and a reflection by the father of one of the victims anchored the page. A second page also gave information on how to contact state legislators and ran a color map pinpointing the locations of the accidents. The newspaper runs a full page of letters daily that sometimes includes original cartoons by readers who are encouraged to "submit painting, collage, computer art, drawing or artwork in any other style" that address Northwest issues.

• *Fort Worth Star-Telegram* op-ed/Sunday editor Bob Davis doesn't shrink when it comes to developing ideas and the presentations to support them, particularly concerning the front page of "The Weekly Review." Indicative of the drama he tries to use to provoke attention was "Campaign '98: The Board Game," which asked readers to identify certain politicians based on recent revelations (Figure 8). Reaction? "My greatest satisfaction is that young hipsters in local coffeehouses were spotted actually playing the game. Cool."

• *The New York Times*, while remaining true to its time-tested traditional editorial page design, has made some adjustments to the op-ed page that it launched in 1970—with

Figure 8

Figure 9

an editorial explaining the concept—and that caught fire and rapidly spread to other newspapers. The page today presents a periodic feature called "Op-Art" that uses photos or illustrations that give a point of view with little need of copy. A stunning example appeared on July 3, 2000, when thirty-five photos were published of individuals displaying the American flag under the headline "What is America?" (Figure 9). In one, two or three words, each made a clear and compelling point of view that needed no other comment or explanation. In all, forty-three words, along with the pictures, covered nearly an entire page.

• *The Charlotte Observer* breaks away from the standard editorial page layout at least several times a year, says the page's editor, Ed Williams. An example is an annual fall two-page photo/editorial package recognizing people who have worked to protect or improve the environment in the Carolinas (Figure 10, first page). "We decided some years ago that our pages would be the authoritative voice on environmental matters in our region," says Williams. The failure of many editorial pages is not recognizing or honoring ordinary citizens, he says. In keeping with that theme, he produces an annual photo/editorial spread on July 4 honoring

Figure 10

Figure 11

Layout and Presentation

Figure 12

Figure 13

people whose efforts make democracy work. Another break with tradition was a page titled, "Living in the age of AIDS" for national AIDS Awareness Day with an editorial, a cartoon and brief essays from seven people in the Charlotte region.

• *The Dallas Morning News* under vice president/editorial page editor Rena Pederson published an unusual treatment of "Dallas Tomorrow" (Figure 11) in which it singled out nineteen city projects with the headline, "It's important for downtown projects to thrive." The editorial urged readers to use the interactive map on the editorial page at the newspaper's Web site, then connect to the Web sites of many of the projects for updates on how they were progressing.

Despite more attention to the look of opinion pages, some note there's still a gap between many editors and designers. Monica Moses, who is on the visual journalism faculty at The Poynter Institute, says that many at the top editorial levels simply like the dignity of the traditional formats and therefore pay little if any attention to possible major changes; she receives few requests for help from her faculty. At the same time, she says, many leaders in the visual field tend not to pay attention to the editorial page because it lacks glamour and far-reaching creative possibilities.

Chapter 7
Layout and Presentation

In a prototype page she designed for this chapter, Moses made simple modifications in the traditional editorial page format (Figure 12). In the biggest and perhaps most controversial change, at the left she suggests a once-a-month "Who We Are" accounting that explains the duties of the editorial board and identifies each member with a small picture and a brief summary of the individual's professional background and political leanings. For the top editorial she uses a headline and pullout quote that support each other. For the second editorial she notes that headline, chart and pullout quote directly convey the key points. For letters she stresses the use of clear, snappy headlines.

She also sketched an op-ed page called "Other Opinions" (Figure 13) made up of syndicated and local columnists. The page would have a daily featured column (assume the illustration fits the copy), and another column, both using pullout quotes to snag the reader, a standalone daily graphic, something she calls a "quick hit with a point of view" followed by a series of quotable quotes.

Moses has a special interest in grabbing the attention of "scanners." "The gist of each opinion piece should be clear at a glance," she said. "Editorials and opinion pieces should be as concise as possible and editing should be ruthless. Several elements on the page, ideally provocative, should be largely visual. Op-ed pages should employ simple tables or other graphics that are rewarding for readers without being labor-intensive."

One of the most extensive and effective efforts to help improve edito-

Figure 14

rial page design was undertaken by Robert H. Bohle of the School of Mass Communication at the University of North Florida. In a series of articles starting in 1987 in *The Masthead,* the quarterly journal of the National Conference of Editorial Writers, Bohle dispensed lively and penetrating practical comments that are as valuable today as they were when presented.

In one piece, entitled "What a good page should look like," (Figure 14), Bohle said the most important rule of good design is to look carefully at the information itself before presenting it. As an example, he presented a page void of illustration that clearly segments editorials starting with a section of "The Facts" then, at

Layout and Presentation

the top piece, giving pros and cons before moving to "Local Opinions" and then "Our Thoughts," or the newspaper's view. This approach allows the reader to better follow the logic, he said.

Whatever course America's daily and weekly newspapers chart in this journey into the visual experience, the opinion pages are likely to remain, at least for a while longer, among the most conservative in terms of change, with continued reliance on strong and clearly crafted views rather than eye-popping design. Considering the historic and fundamental mission of editorials and opinion columns as differentiated from the presentation of news, maybe that's the way it should be— slow but steady.

Chapter 8

In the Cage

By Susan Albright

In the cage. A small, confined space where restlessness builds, passion seethes and tempers flare.

But we're talking editorial departments here, right? The Ivory Tower, and all that?

Combine the two clashing images and, oddly enough, you have it about right. The editorial cage is both a cauldron of commentary and a lonely writer's den. Its quirky inhabitants, willingly separated from their newsroom compatriots by The Great Church/State Wall, nestle perfectly into this seemingly paradoxical environment; they've found their niche, an odd milieu that requires a wide range of seemingly contradictory traits.

Editorial writers come in any number of shapes, sizes, ages and genders—particularly these days, since newspapers have awakened to the benefits of diversifying their once male, pale editorial staffs. The trick for those who choose, guide and nur-

About the author

Susan Albright

Susan Albright has been editor of the editorial pages at the *Star Tribune* in Minneapolis since 1993 and led the editorial pages of the *Arizona Daily Star* from 1985 to 1993. Her staff, which engages in several enterprise projects each year, has earned numerous national awards. Albright served as president of the National Conference of Editorial Writers in 1999 and as a juror for the Pulitzer Prizes in Journalism in 1998 and 1999. She has appeared on National Public Radio's "All Things Considered" and as a regional commentator on public television's "The NewsHour With Jim Lehrer." She holds a master's degree from the S.I. Newhouse School of Public Communications, Syracuse University.

ture them is discerning whether any would-be opiner's assorted qualities add up to an interesting whole and whether it would enhance what's already in the room. As Philip Geyelin, Pulitzer Prize winner and editorial page editor of the *St. Petersburg Times*, says, "You look for your weaknesses and soft spots and try to find people who will fill those."

Next to choosing the right newspaper (and publisher), choosing the right staff is the most critical decision an editorial page editor or station manager must make. Senate candidates and legislative bills come and go. So do tough calls, ethical dilemmas, libelous letters and assorted other journalistic decision points. But your writers come back, every day, every month—sometimes every decade. They speak for you, for each other, for your newspaper or your broadcast outlet. You want that cage filled with the right lions and tigers.

Who might that be? Seasoned reporters? Think-tankers? Poly-sci Ph.D.s? Ex-copy editors, activists, twenty-somethings? Hoary experts?

Maybe.

In *Newspaper Days*, H.L. Mencken described the editorial enterprise as consisting of the managing editor, aided by "two or three ancient hulks who were unfit for any better duty—copy readers promoted from the city-room to get rid of them, alcoholic writers of local histories and forgotten novels, former managing editors who had come to grief on other papers, and a miscellany of decayed lawyers, college professors and clergymen with whispered pasts. . . . No editorial writer was ever applied to for a loan,

or invited to an office booze-party."

Well, now. Vintage over-the-top Mencken to be sure, but talk to a few veteran editorial page editors and some will tell you that there was more than a kernel of truth in his curmudgeonly description; some editors viewed the editorial page as a "dumping ground for hacks or burnouts," as one editorialist put it. Sort of like the police sergeant's desk, where washed-up Clint Eastwood types were sent if they goofed up on the street or got tired feet.

Geyelin was determined that his shop in St. Petersburg would be different. He has systematically collected an eclectic group that includes several writers from outside journalism. He looks for "bright people who can write and think, and who care about issues." His writers include Robyn Blumner, a lawyer formerly with the American Civil Liberties Union who was a source for the staff on First Amendment issues. Geyelin persuaded her first to write columns on First Amendment subjects and, eventually, to make the leap to editorial writing. Now she's also a syndicated columnist. Among his other non-journalism hires were an anthropologist, an African-American community college English teacher and an author/professor/NPR commentator who after joining the staff spent three months of each year writing her editorials from England. Geyelin says he can't imagine not having people like these on his staff. He believes editors who hire only journalists "sometimes miss out on the complexities of the real world." What these people have in common are good minds, a sense of outrage and a wide range of life experiences and expertise.

Chapter 8
In the Cage

Joe Stroud once told me that an editorial writer ought to be the kind of person who'd show up at the morning meeting with a fist-pounding, resounding, "We can't let the bastards get away with it!"

Amen. Stroud, who led the *Detroit Free Press'* editorial staff for decades before exchanging editing pleasures for three columns a week and a teaching schedule, had the essence right: Editorial writers must have, at least somewhere in their bones, a commitment to justice that makes them want to cry out. It can take a lot of forms; it can come from left or right. It can be passionate or quiet. It can even be developed. But it has to be there.

It's not, however, enough. You also need a social conscience, solid reporting techniques, an abiding intellectual curiosity, energy, an ethical center, the ability to make quick sense of an issue, an open mind, analytical skills, a firm spine, the ability to harness adrenaline in a hurry . . . and writing talent, at a minimum.

A sense of humor doesn't hurt. And unless you have a writer for every subject (hah!), you need a lifelong learner: the sort of person who takes classes in poetry writing, statistics or history—for fun.

If you're in a shop that's fortunate enough to have several writers, the equation gets even more interesting. You can create a department with complementary strengths, interests and skills. Our department at the *Star Tribune* is lucky enough, for example, to contain a writer who rhapsodizes about the yearly appearance of her magnolia blossoms and another who can wax with equal enthusiasm about the intricacies of tax increment financing. They work next to a jazz aficionado with a philosophy degree and a brain for economics; an ex-investigative projects editor who has fallen in love with the Alaskan wilderness and golf; an editor/writer who's also an actor and runner, training for his second marathon. And so on. Together we've learned that everything in life is potential grist; the whole package matters, not just the part that follows politics and public policy.

Finally, there's something to be said for maturity and a broad knowledge base. When building a staff, it's important to include in your candidate pool seasoned reporters who are itching to write opinion. Other backgrounds bring richness and expertise to the table. But don't overlook reporters—lively ones, to be sure—because they walk in the door with journalistic ethics, reporting skills and a solid work ethic built into their skeletons.

Steve Berg, an editorial writer for the *Star Tribune,* once observed that he'd kept his opinions to himself for years covering politics and national affairs, and eventually found himself ready to move "from description to prescription." It's a neat way of saying that when you've observed a lot, learned a lot, written a lot, it's natural to have formed some opinions. Moving to editorial writing makes sense.

Not all reporters are like that. Some come looking for the job, but can't quite let loose once they have it. You have to find those who eventually can, and let them loose.

Letting loose?

The concept of letting loose may seem contrary to the art of writing

Chapter 8
In the Cage

THE VOICE OF THE INSTITUTION. What a mantle to don!

No big deal for some, who easily assume their voice is the institution's by dint of their hiring. For others, it can be initially (or terminally) inhibiting, even stifling. For most it takes a while to forget it's on your back—whether you're coming from the newsroom, academe or the street.

Once worn lightly, though, the mantle of the institution provides nothing short of freedom. While I've heard of editors who believe each editorial must be edited to have the exact same voice—as though one person had written every editorial for decades—I haven't seen that philosophy work. Editorials work best when writers form their own analogies, use their own cadences—and tap into their own sense of justice. It's the job of the editor to set the boundaries of the institution's persona—and to let it sing.

The singing, of course, must occur not only within the boundaries of the newspaper or TV station's political philosophy, but also within the boundaries of five hundred words (or whatever). And in some corner of each writer's head is also the awareness that he is writing not just one person's view, but the distilled essence—couched, to be sure, in one writer's voice—of the vaunted EDITORIAL BOARD.

"Letting loose" within all these boundaries is surprisingly easy for those who come to do it well. It's a matter of harnessing your own knowledge, crafting your own argument, but doing so with full awareness of both the institution's editorial traditions and the conversations that led to your writing.

Which brings us to the editorial board meeting. Those who've worked in solitary splendor have been known to disdain the whole concept as one that can only dilute opinion, turning sharpness into mush. Well done, however, it is a thing of beauty. Instead of the dilution of opinion, it is the distillation. The writer who leaves the room with a mission for the day is a person armed with a clear direction, plus all the ideas that led to that direction. You are ready to tackle the subject in your own way.

Otherwise you don't write. Howell Raines, editor of *The New York Times'* editorial page, told writers at a Poynter Institute seminar, "If it feels boring to you as you write it, it is. Get another topic." He believes editorials should inform and delight: "No eat-your-peas editorials—the kind that say to readers, 'Eat this nice warm bowl of policy with your breakfasts. It's your duty as a citizen.'" Similarly, Pulitzer Prize winner Paul Greenberg, editorial page editor of the *Arkansas Democrat-Gazette*, has long coached editorial writers to pass up the "duty editorial." It's a killer—a killer of energy, of passion, of everything that makes an editorial worth reading.

Oh, yes, certain events will demand that you write. The Oklahoma City bombing, your city's team winning the Super Bowl, the election of a wrestler-cum-talk-show-host to the governorship of Minnesota. But unless you—or your staff as a group—can muster a clear, convincing argument, a cogent sentiment or an elegiac essay, it won't sing.

You may argue that sometimes you have a duty to muster. That's true. Just don't write until you do.

The decision

The concept of an editorial board

Chapter 8
In the Cage

arriving at a clear point of view is a mystery to anyone who hasn't achieved it. We're not going to demystify it here; that might ruin its magic. But it's important to talk about what an editorial board session should and should not be.

It should not be a search for absolute consensus, the kind where every person must agree with every nuance, where all life is driven from the issue. At the other end of the spectrum, it should not be editorial position by fiat. At its best, it is a discussion among prepared thinkers—people who arrive with ideas and hand them out in a way that respects both colleagues and expertise.

Joel Kramer, my first publisher at the *Star Tribune,* had a way of looking at editorial decision-making that has been a guiding principle for me. The point of an editorial board meeting isn't for everyone to agree. We're talking about a daily newspaper or nightly news broadcast, after all. It is, rather, to reach a point, on any given issue, where the group realizes that it has arrived at the right position for the institution to take. That involves an awareness of past positions and the reasons for them. It involves listening especially hard to the person in the room with the most knowledge of the subject at hand. It means identifying underlying principles and tossing aside nuances that don't really matter. Ultimately, for each individual present, it means not a fight to win an argument but a search for a position that best reflects this group's best thinking, keeping in mind what it collectively has said in the past.

"Try to make sure all points of view on an issue are debated, since the resulting editorial will be less persuasive if it fails to acknowledge opposing opinions," advises Robert Barnard, retired editorial page editor of *The Courier-Journal* in Louisville, Kentucky, and former NCEW president. "Even 'old' issues need an occasional review, lest staleness succeed one-time vigor. And few things are more damaging than the perception that you see little need for continuing research."

Having said all this, someone else is always in the room, whether literally or figuratively. And *he* must be reckoned with.

The owner

Oh, yes. The owner. The general manager. The publisher. Whoever. Someone up there is accountable for all this. Still another voice, and one with ultimate authority. How to deal with him? (Well, it's usually a him, though life changes. Until it does, *he* will do).

The owner, of course, can do what he likes. The owner may be a person or a chain. He or it may be local or distant, embedded in the community or imposed upon it.

Today, mergers and acquisitions spell frequent change. Danielle Smith of the *Calgary Herald* tells the story of her newspaper's recent shift from political left to right. In that case, Smith said, newspaper mogul Conrad Black wanted each of his newly acquired editorial pages to reflect the community in which it lived. It was decided that Calgary was more conservative than the paper, so the editorial page changed. Hence, the staff changed. The fact that the *Herald* was

Chapter 8
In the Cage

later sold yet again hasn't led, so far, to further change.

And so it goes. Owners can do what they like. Publishers can, too, theoretically—although they, too, are frequently constrained if they're paid by a chain.

In truth, all sorts of arrangements can work. What matters is that whoever supervises the editorial page is in sync with the editorial page editor. That the station manager and his editorial writer are in sync. That they respect each other and what came before them—and that they agree to explain major changes to the reader.

The editorial page editor must advocate both from the editorial writers to the publisher (or whomever) and from the publisher to the editorial writers. The rub often comes when a publisher, hearing all sorts of input from the community, wonders whether his editorial writers are on the right track. It is the editorial page editor's job to be the person between staff and publisher/owner, to advocate, as one editor put it, "both up and down."

It is my feeling that everything works best when the publisher, having hired an in-sync editorial page editor, lets the operation work largely by itself. He must be knowledgeable; he must ascertain regularly that he is comfortable with what's going on with his staff. But there is much to be said for honoring expertise, for allowing freedom within the boundaries. What publisher really has time to study up on the intricacies of funding health care? Of deciphering energy deregulation? Of sorting out First Amendment vs. Fourth Amendment tugs?

The philosophy

Leaving aside dramatic shifts like Calgary's, what clearly makes the most sense to any given paper's readers, or any given TV station's viewers, is a reasonably consistent way of looking at the world over time.

For that to occur, everyone involved—owner, publisher, editorial page editor and writer—must think of the enterprise as being of them but not them.

The institutional voice has a persona all its own, a personality with a set of values. And those values serve to inform any current crop of writers. Often these values can be traced to a particularly vibrant owner or editorialist from the past, someone who put a sharp imprint on the paper.

It's not that an editorial writer or editor would want to go around today imagining how Old So & So would think about an issue. It's rather that the positions and personality of the past are acknowledged, respected and dealt with.

Authentic writing has to come from within. Writers can't focus on, or be overly concerned with, what the founder would think—or, for that matter, what their boss will think. Once in the office cubicle, at the laptop or staring at the home computer in the middle of the night, the writer must make the issue his own.

It's the duty of his editor to help him become the best he can be at making his arguments—not to be like his colleague in the next office, not to slavishly repeat the publisher's arguments, not to echo H.L. Mencken or William Allen White, but to tap his own strengths, employ his own

In the Cage

analysis, his own sense of justice and his own style.

But if you allow (let alone encourage) that, some worry, won't the editorials lack a discernible identity? Won't it look like a jumble of different styles? Won't it confuse?

Actually, it will simply look alive.

Imagine a person with only one dimension—a person who wears the same demeanor, the same clothes, and who speaks with the same tone of voice all the time everywhere he goes. Now imagine living with this person day after day, year after year.

How much more interesting is the person who expresses myriad aspects of himself—through everything from the hat he chooses to the way he walks and talks. Just as a person can be alternately serious, analytical, amusing and profound, so can an editorial page.

Just as an individual editorial writer can rave about a rock concert he heard the night before and five minutes later launch into a critique of Vladimir Putin's presidency, an editorial page can feature sharp commentary on Chechnya at the top, support for a family-leave bill underneath and a rhapsody on autumn oak leaves at the bottom. During the week, and over a year, it should take on a rhythm as well.

Such an approach is rich for readers; it also keeps writers awake.

There is nothing quite so deadening as inexorability. Even in a job as meaningful and as expressive as editorial writing, the daily deadline can become the daily duty.

The latest bill in the legislature,

the latest City Hall budget, the latest pronouncement from the governor—all are obvious editorial subjects. And a practiced editorial writer will be tempted to take them on one by one, to do some interviews, come up with a reasoned position, build an argument and advance it.

If he's lucky, he'll get excited about the issue once into it, and the resulting editorial will ring with purpose and commitment. The danger lies in doing too many editorials that arise from external events, from news stories or others' suggestions. The writer who stays fresh is a writer who plans ahead—who finds a rhythm in which he can choose the occasional project, who finds a way to fit in editorials about things that are enduringly meaningful to him, not to the editor who put something on page one the night before.

It has been said that at the core of leadership is energy. And if they want to lead, editorial writers must find ways to infuse energy into their thinking and writing. They must tackle issues that get their juices flowing—and never be satisfied with the merely competent editorial. Well, almost never. There are Fridays, after all. But your sustained energy will depend on the approach you take to the afternoon, to the week, to the year.

You must control it—at least a little.

Out of the grind

Projects, paradoxically, energize everyone involved. Doing something original and important, something that takes time to put together—and especially something no one else has thought much about—seems on the

In the Cage

surface to be a sure drainer. How could you possibly do a series on the county's response to child abuse, for example, when you barely have time to respond to the Irish peace plan today and the president's gun-control proposal tomorrow?

Oddly enough, you can—and you must. Otherwise you're always responding, always writing about someone else's pet interest, someone else's passion—on someone else's schedule.

It isn't easy—not for a big shop, certainly not for a small shop. It is necessary though, both for your readers and for you.

Boldness and creativity help. When Maria Henson began to see that Kentucky women had little support from judges and the courts after being abused at home, she saw a project much larger than an editorial or two. But what to do? Her editor at the *Lexington Herald-Leader*, David Holwerk, supported the effort by doing whatever it took. If the page had just one editorial on a given day, it was in service to something the staff knew was important. If others had to carry the load sometimes, it helped the cause. Next time it would be someone else's project, someone else's turn to dig in. Henson (who is now deputy editorial page editor of the *Austin American Statesman)* worked on "To Have and to Harm: Kentucky's Failure to Protect Women From the Men Who Beat Them" for sixteen months. The editorials appeared over the course of a year. For Henson, Holwerk and Company the result was the 1992 Pulitzer Prize for Editorial Writing—and, more important, critical changes for abused women in Kentucky.

Similarly, John Bersia of the *Orlando Sentinel* spent two thousand hours on his series, "Fleeced in Florida," about lending practices that victimized immigrants, students, military personnel and others. "They were taking advantage of people who didn't have a voice," Bersia told editorial writers at the 2000 convention of the National Conference of Editorial Writers in Seattle. "We gave them a voice."

To do so, Bersia conducted over one thousand interviews, one-third of them with victims. His colleagues largely held down the editorial fort, with Bersia contributing to the daily editorial output only occasionally.

Like Henson's project, Bersia's grew. "After the first editorials, the editor said, 'We're going to do this bigger, better and bolder,'" he said. So Bersia started again. It took a raft of county ordinances, one hundred fifteen or so editorials and two legislative sessions before the state acted. "There were times I was away from the office for weeks at a time," he said.

The result was concrete—and gratifying. When the governor signed a bill that reined in the industry, he publicly presented Bersia with a signing pen. The Pulitzer board awarded Bersia the 2000 editorial writing prize. Congress held hearings, and journalists in other states took note and began writing.

Most of all, the *Orlando Sentinel*, through Bersia's creative and dogged work, made a difference in the lives of voiceless Floridians.

It's the same with endorsement season. Like an enterprise project, it

Chapter 8
In the Cage

takes you away from the day-to-day grind. It's invigorating, if a pain in the neck. It provides a service to readers, and it puts you face to face with the candidates. Those interchanges will inform your writing, will provide you with sources for the future, and will give you a window on what candidates are hearing on the stump.

And, of course, it breaks your routine. A year of editorial writing without agendas, projects or endorsements is like a school year of classes and homework—but no school play, no recitals, no Valentine's Day, no science fair.

Don't try it for long. Unless you're in it for the short-term, treat this job as a marathon, not a sprint.

The management thing

This is for bosses only.

You can foster all of the above, hire terrific people, insist on producing important projects, stress proactivity and reward powerful writing—and still have a sour, unhappy, contentious staff. Your life and theirs will be meaningful but miserable. And it will show on your pages.

You need to lead, and you need to manage. That frequently takes more skills than most journalists possess—especially since most of us came from newsrooms, which reward good writing and editing and promote those who do them well—without training in managing time, let alone people. Yet here you are, and manage you must.

If your early newsroom editors were anything like mine, they wanted you to prove you belonged in the august realm of their newspaper by doing everything fast and right. Nothing else mattered. Not civility, not fairness in interpersonal dealings, certainly not the need to acknowledge or, heaven forbid, compliment.

Now, all these years later, you've proved you can do things fast and right. But you're running a department and you need to know some things. You need to know how to lead, how to help your staff lead. You need energy, empathy, focus and good humor.

"The hard part," says Robert Barnard, "besides setting examples you'd like others to follow, is remembering not to take staffers for granted. We all welcome encouragement when we've done well, and shouldn't have to wait for payroll review time to learn we've been falling short. Such surprises hurt everybody—very much including their supervisor, you."

Yes, you have to be as demanding as those curmudgeons of yore, but preferably without being a boor. This Top 10 list might help.

1. Don't get bogged down in office bureaucracy (far easier said than done). Write often and write well.

2. Don't assume your best writers are your most confident. Tell them they're terrific—often, and exactly why. (Remember the study about competence? The incompetent thought they were doing fine, no problem, and the most competent were frequently plagued with self-doubt.)

3. Do those dratted performance reviews on time. Your staff wants your feedback, and they deserve the raise now.

In the Cage

4. Confront the mail when it hits your desk. And don't just push it around.

5. Confront problems when they hit your radar. They don't generally cure themselves; they fester.

6. Effectively advocate for your staff—with your boss, with the newsroom, with the public, with the press.

7. Get out of the office.

8. Bring doughnuts now and then.

9. Trust your staff, and let them know you do.

10. Hire as though you'll be spending twenty years with them; you just might.

Above all, forget the editor-in-the-movies stereotype, except the parts about 1) the necessity for both journalistic and managerial courage and 2) your duty to be tough with the green pencil. The buck stops with you.

If that doesn't put enough pressure on you, remember: This is no job for a sprinter. Take care of yourself, or you won't be there for anyone else.

Chapter 9

Time Management

By Nancy Q. Keefe

Time is to clock as mind is to brain. The clock or watch somehow contains the time. And yet time refuses to be bottled up like a genie stuffed in a lamp. Whether it flows as sand or turns on wheels within wheels, time escapes irretrievably, while we watch. Even when the bulbs of the hourglass shatter, when darkness withholds the shadow from the sundial, when the mainspring winds down so far that the clock hands hold still as death, time itself keeps on. The most we can hope a watch to do is mark that progress. And since time sets its own tempo, like a heartbeat or an ebb tide, timepieces don't really keep time. They just keep up with it, if they're able.

—from *Longitude* by Dava Sobel

So true, agreed Mindy Cameron, editorial page editor of *The Seattle Times*.

"You can't make more time," she

About the author

Nancy Q. Keefe

Nancy Q. Keefe spent about forty years in the daily newspaper business, first at *The Berkshire Eagle* in her hometown of Pittsfield, Massachusetts, later the old *New York World Telegram & Sun* and then at the Gannett group of dailies in suburban Westchester County, New York. She found the job ideal because of her short attention span, which means she has to finish something by the end of the day or will lose interest. And as a world-class procrastinator, the daily deadline provided the prod to get the job done. She retired in 1998 and continues to live by the maxim: Carpe diem.

Time Management

said, "so place a great value on it. Make maximum use of that time." Even better is the suggestion she heard about developing a "new relationship to time."

"It's really a rich one to think about, and I thought a lot about it," she said.

Probably we all should begin there, acknowledging that time can be a problem (there's never enough time), a tyrant (those daily deadlines), a will-o'-the-wisp (where does the time go?), a thief (how fast children grow up, how quickly we grow older, time snatching the golden days). Having recognized that, we can try thinking about it differently.

Cameron began developing her new relationship to time by saying "no" to the usual way of doing things.

For Jim Boyd of the Minneapolis *Star Tribune,* a way to get a handle on managing time is, "Don't touch paper twice if you can avoid it. Touch each piece of copy only once."

Maura Casey at *The Day* in New London, Connecticut, manages by getting "totally focused on work," she said. "I almost don't talk to people at work. I just work at work."

Three different people, three different approaches. Yours will be different yet, especially if you work in the broadcast side of editorials. From the start, that's always about time, not space.

"I get sixty seconds, give or take a few," said Neil Heinen, editorial director of WISC-TV in Madison, Wisconsin. "That's one hundred seventy-five words. So they have to be the best one hundred seventy-five words."

It takes time to write that short and say anything. On top of that, as Chuck Stokes points out:

"There's just never enough time in the day to wear all the different hats we have to wear to get the job done." As the high-profile editorial and public affairs director at WXYZ-TV of Detroit, with a weekend show and a stint as National Conference of Editorial Writers president, he's had to play a lot of roles. "But knowing there's just so much time," he added, "you itemize that time and force yourself to get it done."

How? Perhaps we first need to realize that we have different internal clocks and rhythms, as well as different demands from paper to paper, from station to station. So we need different approaches to manage time for ourselves in our own places.

Kay Semion, for instance, knows this about herself: "I write best in the morning, so I schedule writing for then and set aside afternoon time for editing letters, essays, research, etc. I try to stick to time frames and limit interruptions." When she was a one-person editorial department in Ann Arbor, Michigan, she'd shut her door during writing times and set her phone for taking messages. If she was interrupted anyway, she said, she'd explain that she was on deadline, which is true all day long for a one-person editorial page staff. And be firm, she urged, because "studies have shown that after a five-minute interruption, it can take you ten minutes to return to the point where you were interrupted."

Vanessa J. Gallman, by contrast, has realized that for her, as editorial page editor at the *Lexington Herald-Leader*

Chapter 9
Time Management

in Kentucky, "it's really better to deal with calls when they come. It's hard for me when I'm writing or on deadline. Then I do let voice mail handle calls. But other times, they stack up and you miss people when you call them back later. So now I try to deal with them when they come and I've found that they don't take so long that way."

Rick Horowitz has an altogether different sense of time. As a syndicated columnist and television commentator, his time is his own, but it's also his livelihood. When he's writing, either for the column, which he files Tuesday morning, or the commentary, which he does Friday, he answers the phone.

"It may not be the most effective thing to do," he admits, "but I talk quickly and say I'll call back." In his defense, he said, "I don't always run downstairs when I hear the mailman come." In 1985, when he fractured his arm playing softball and had the arm in a kind of cast for sixteen months, he did not miss a deadline. It was before electronic filing, too. He folded, collated and mailed every column because he knew he must meet his deadline.

"I get the day-to-day done," he said wistfully, "but I'm not as good at the long-range things." That may be true of many of us, but we can learn from one another.

As you see how various people have developed strategies and tactics, you will be able to sort through what will work for you personally and for your shop. Take up what works and jettison the rest. It will be your first success in managing time.

When she became editorial page editor, Mindy Cameron saw how "the long-standing tradition of the editorial board" ate up time.

"The interests out there in the community believed they needed the editorial board meeting. I kind of went along with that for a while," she said, "then realized it was taking a lot of time. Gradually, we went to individual writers doing their own reporting the old-fashioned way, and saying *no* more and more often, not doing nearly as many editorial board meetings. I think that's a message I try to deliver. And people say: 'Oh, you mean you say *no?*' Yes. You're in charge. Say *no.*"

The *Journal-News,* the successor newspaper to the group of dailies published by the Gannett Company in suburban New York where I used to work, found another way to save the editorial board from meeting with everybody who showed up at the door. The editorial page invites members of community organizations to write a column called "Who We Are." It runs four hundred to five hundred words, introducing special-interest groups to readers and editors. At the same time, it provides the editorial page with a different voice.

Saying *no* to editorial board meetings doesn't mean that you deny access to people in your community. At *The Seattle Times,* the editorial page staff goes out to see the community movers and shakers on their turf and gets a firsthand sense of what they do. At the appropriate time, the editorial page reports and comments on them, often in "editorial notebooks, short signed pieces that run in the editorial column," Cameron said. She sees them as "a way to inject personality into the institutional bloodstream of that venerable space," as

Time Management

she wrote in *The Masthead*.

When really big news comes to town, such as the World Trade Organization, the editorial writers are "out on the streets taking it all in," Cameron said. She'd envisioned a series of editorial notebooks for the WTO meeting.

Instead, as the circus in Seattle unfolded in December 1999, the writers produced short essays that captured the moments on the opening day. As the week turned violent, the page turned to more traditional ways of handling opinion, using editorials, letters and columns to show what went wrong.

Going out takes too much time? Not necessarily, as Vanessa Gallman found in Lexington.

"I like, I prefer getting out," she said. "It helps me see their world. We actually decided to take the time to let the editorial writers report—go out and check out the chicken farms, go to meetings. Once we made that commitment, it required more of a juggle for the three writers and me. But what's amazing is it makes it almost easier. I'm not sure why. People know they're going to get a turn to go out, and others step up and fill the void when one is out reporting. Still, I never suspected they would produce more and better."

One reason is that when you go out to look at something firsthand, it becomes more vivid for you, and it becomes yours. You can write about it more quickly and eloquently than you ever could by staying in the office and writing from dry research.

Sometimes, though, you have to stay in and have the editorial board

meeting, especially if your newspaper or station endorses candidates for political office. But you don't have to provide every candidate with a solo act on your stage. By planning well before election season, you can schedule candidates for the same office to appear at the same time. This cuts in half the amount of time you have to spend listening to them and has a big added advantage. They have to confront each another, and deal with the same issues and the same charges when they're in the same room. No talking past each another, as they often do when they come in alone.

You could streamline it even more by doing your own variation on the way we at Gannett in Westchester County, New York, handled candidates for judge one year. About twenty-five people were running for judicial office at the county and state levels in our suburban coverage area. Seeing them separately would have taken forever and been deadly boring besides, because judicial candidates can't discuss cases or indicate how they would rule on certain matters that might come before them. Yet voters rely heavily on newspaper endorsements for judges because most voters have no idea who the candidates are.

We invited all the candidates to come on one day—Columbus Day, when the courts are closed. We said we'd sit as an editorial board from 10 A.M. to 2 P.M. The candidates could stop by and talk with us for as long as they liked. We'd discuss no cases, only the philosophy of law, we told them.

They all showed up at ten and stayed till two, talking about every-

Chapter 9
Time Management

thing from the framers of the Constitution to their own sense of what is meant by "the rule of law." Some were eloquent, others were pompous. Some made jokes, others hardly spoke. Out of it we got a wonderful sense of who they were.

Organizing the day and listening to the candidates required a major investment of our time. But it took less time than seeing them individually, and it paid off handsomely. We made our best endorsements because we could sense who among them had good judicial temperament.

Sometimes you have to invest time to save it in the long run. The key is understanding how you use time, what you're good at, what your weaknesses are and what your staff's strengths and weaknesses are.

Specialists in time management say you need to understand that you function differently at different times of the day. Think about how you work; even keep a log for a week to discover your pattern of energy and lethargy. Use the information to schedule your day. If, like Kay Semion, you write better in the morning, do it then. Use the afternoon for routine tasks, such as sorting through letters to the editor.

Dan Radmacher of *The Charleston Gazette* in West Virginia suggests mixing "things that require thought and things that don't, so you don't get burnout." He added, "You're still thinking, but not at the same rate."

If you're a slow starter, experts say it may be your eating patterns. A good breakfast with plenty of carbohydrates will keep you going for a while, but then the sugars fade because your high levels of energy burn them quickly. For some people, a mid-morning snack will replenish the energy. But if carbohydrate-loading isn't for you, consider eating protein at breakfast, such as eggs, to delay the drop in energy.

See what works for you. No one size—or one menu—suits all. But one universal does seem to hold true. A big lunch makes you sleepy, apparently because it takes blood from your brain to your digestive system. The siesta is a wonderful concept but unfortunately not part of our culture. So eat lightly and stay away from alcohol at lunch if you want to accomplish anything in the afternoon.

Don't skip lunch—or the lunch break—entirely, though. You may think you have no time, but if you try to work through the day with no breaks, you'll fade before the end of the afternoon. Semion suggests "a mid-day personal break." For her, it's "usually a racquetball game or workout or lunch with a personal friend. It refreshes my mind for the afternoon."

Studies back her up. Eating right and taking breaks help you extend the amount of quality time by a lot. Find the pattern that suits your body clock.

Another factor that can keep us from getting the most of the day is procrastination: "the thief of time," as the poet Edward Young called it.

Analysts say we procrastinate because we overplan or we can't bring ourselves to confront an issue or we seek perfection. Overplanning causes paralysis. Confronting issues is what we're paid to do. Perfectionism is not possible this side of the grave. So get on with it.

Chapter 9
Time Management

Radmacher, as editorial page editor at *The Charleston Gazette*, has to do nearly everything. He and the editor of the paper write all the editorials. The copy desk paginates. But the rest, including handling many aspects of the paper's Web site, is up to him. He can't procrastinate, so he's got a "kind of system," he said.

"I have a pretty good idea of what I need to do every day. When I come in, I tend to do the same things in the same order. First, I find the columns for the next day. That gets me on the wires, a kind of a wake-up. Then I pick out cartoons. Then I start reading papers and hopefully get inspired to write an editorial. I research and write the edit—or two." He doesn't put off confrontation or wait for perfection to strike. "I save editing letters for late," he adds.

For some, paperwork is the instrument of procrastination. Paperwork is a fact of life but need not control our lives. Jim Boyd suggests that as soon as any piece of paper comes to you:

"Make your decision right now. Don't touch paper twice if you can avoid it. When I opened letters [to the editor], I chose them." The right instincts develop, he said, and so you should "do it now and not go back, not second-guess yourself. Keep going. Touch each piece of copy once.

"This spills over to other things as well. If you're in a small shop and have to deal with invoices and other such things, do it now," he said. "Get invited to a dinner? Decide. Put it on the calendar now if you say *yes*. Don't put it aside and think about it later. Even if you're in the middle of an op-ed piece when it comes, decide now and do it."

The same holds true if you head a large staff. Decide what to do with each piece of paper as it comes in. Then, get rid of it. Whether you pass it along, file it, sign it, revise it or throw it out, take action on it right away. But no fair filing everything and saying you've dealt with it.

For Maura Casey in New London, having an intense career and being a mom means she has to focus in on the task at hand. Besides just working at work, as she puts it, and not hanging out having coffee, "I always bring home stuff to read. Even during TV commercials, you can read. On Sunday, when I read *The New York Times*, I'm always circling stuff for edits—part of me is always working— so Monday I always have topics."

If she's researching a complicated issue, she does it over time.

"Every day I put in at least a half hour on that topic," she said. "I read and make at least a couple phone calls."

When Mindy Cameron has a topic she wants to write about but hasn't thought it through, she sets it aside till she's driving home or cooking or doing something else. That's "soak time," as she calls it, "time for germination of the idea."

Sometimes, like Alice and the looking-glass, you have to go away from a thing to get back to it. But that's not procrastinating. That's being creative.

Even at the end of a long day, you can still accomplish something. Casey said, "Before I go to bed, I make a list of people to call the next day and throw it in my bag."

Try to get to the point where having a list and checking off the things

Time Management

you've done is more satisfying than your tendency to procrastinate.

To keep others from infecting us with procrastination, try this: Schedule meetings at 11 a.m. Kay Semion has "found that the most efficient, shortest meetings occur then because nearly everyone wants to get out to go to lunch."

If procrastination afflicts you or a colleague, causing difficulties day to day or on long-range projects, set intermediate deadlines. Many of us in this business perform well only when deadline looms. Time management specialists call it "the deadline high" because making deadline is immensely satisfying and can give a big rush of adrenaline. Intermediate deadlines may not provide the big rush, but they do prevent the breathless dash to the finish that can wreck both the project and morale.

It's really not procrastination, you say, but true lack of time that causes the frantic finishes.

OK. Try getting up earlier. This is not just a facetious response but a simple way of "creating" more time. Specialists point out that if you get up one hour earlier every day for a year, you have given yourself ten more working weeks. A few caveats, though. You need to use the time well, not just to drag things out longer. Use the hour for something specific and special, such as research for a long-range project that will have a definite end, an early-morning run, outside reading to enrich your thinking and writing.

If you decide to get up early, you'll probably find it brutal at first and you may be tired during the day. But you'll find it easier every day. Soon you'll be awake before the alarm goes off and your body will adjust. Still, you ought to go to bed earlier at night, because sleep deprivation, a major affliction of Americans in our time, is not the way to make effective use of the extra time.

Perhaps it's not putting things off so much as not letting things go that keeps your editorial page staff from performing well.

When Vanessa Gallman became editorial page editor, she found that she needed better production help to get her pages out on time and looking good. She knew she had to set up a system, including naming a person to handle the details and to take care of relationships with copy desk.

"Finding the right person for that, instead of me," Gallman said, "that was a kind of a first letting-go." It wasn't easy, she acknowledges, but it was crucial. She carried it a step further and "also found out when you're not in the office, the pages come out! So you get to the point where you trust the people while you're away. You keep in touch but don't get neurotic about it."

"I was not that indispensable," she said with a laugh.

Semion as a one-person shop, was, unfortunately, indispensable. Still, she had to have a life outside the editorial page, so she came up with ways to keep control without having to oversee every aspect of the page, among them, a flexible page design. The editorial column allowed for fillers, such as a list of addresses of elected officials, if the editorials didn't use all the room. The letters column could take a policy statement, condensed as needed. The local essay at the bottom of the page could take art or bold-faced quotes. The two daily syndicated columnists on the op-ed page ran on a schedule with a back-up list that the copy desk could choose from.

Unless you're a one-person staff, or the rest of your staff is the editor-in-chief or station manager, you need to delegate to leave yourself time for the big picture—planning, thinking, writing the pieces that you are good at. As for the rest, management experts suggest these guidelines:

• Decide what to delegate by figuring out what you do best and what others on the staff do best. Select the people who can carry out important jobs without your help. Consider what inexperienced staff members may be good at and assign appropriate jobs to them, making it clear that you will coach, encourage and supervise while they learn.

• When you delegate, give over the whole job, whether it is daily dealings with the copy desk or management of a long-range project. If you are a staff member being assigned a job, ask your editor for the whole job. Studies show that we all find it more satisfying to work on a single task than on fragments of many tasks. The one job becomes our total responsibility, with our name on it, as it were. We will, of course, want to do it brilliantly.

• In making the assignment, explain it, put it in context of the whole editorial effort, make clear what information you want back. Then let go. Don't hover, but do let your staff know you will help if they need it. And if the assistant makes a mistake, not out of laziness but from doing something new, point out that it's a great way to learn. The best shortstops in baseball make errors because they try for every ball hit in their direction. But they also make brilliant plays. So it is with all of us. We shine when we go for the hard ones.

• Finally, when the assistant does the job well, be sure to give credit that all the others hear.

If you find it difficult to delegate, step back and ask yourself why. Not enough time to explain the job? Invest the time. It will pay off later. Fear of mistakes? That's how we all learn. Watch toddlers learning to walk. How many times do they fall and get up before they can walk across a room?

Afraid they're not up to it? Maybe they haven't been tested. If you delegate it, they will perform.

Fear of giving up some authority? How much authority do you need? You may be surrendering some intermediate marching orders, but you never give up the responsibility for a job well done in the end. When you as the editor or editorial supervisor delegate well, you are doing the whole job effectively.

If you think delegating will make you superfluous, don't worry. You'll have plenty to do, and in your moments of leisure you can take credit for building and training such a good staff.

Then, to be sure you are getting all that you can out of yourself, here are some additional suggestions:

• Plan your day the night before and list the items in the order of importance. If you can, do the most important first, then the second most important, and so on. If other factors, such as production demands, interfere, you have to accommodate those. But stick to your list as much as you can. You won't finish everything, but you will get more done this way.

• Overplan your days, taking a page from Parkinson's law book: Projects tend to take all the time allocated to them. If you have only one thing to do, it will take all day. If you schedule ten projects, you may complete eight. The only hazard is that when others want something done they tend to ask a busy person. You may find yourself with even more work. Also learn to say *no* nicely.

• Should you then find yourself with five extra minutes, Rick Horowitz suggests finding better verbs. "Verbs are powerful," he reminds us. "Or take ten percent off a piece in progress or a piece you've done. You wrote six hundred words? Cut sixty. Ask yourself, "What's it about?"'

• Take a hint from the broadcast people: "Pick a point, Neil," Heinen tells himself. Make it and get out.

Let's face it, though. News people, including editorial writers, in print and broadcast, are not like other people. We're not going to become so organized that someone would write a book about our work habits. We like reacting to the unscheduled, the unpredictable. That's why we do what we do—it's called breaking news. We have short attention spans. That's why we do this job. It's new every day. So we can't worry our time management practices to a high polish or fit them on a flow chart.

Take from here what fits you, at least as comfortably as the jacket you keep in the office in case the governor comes. And don't fret over the rest. But don't file it, either.

Broadcast Editorials: Where Seconds Count

"I don't know if it's really all that different," said Chuck Stokes, TV editorial director in Detroit, contrasting broadcast editorials and print. "I think we're all just always racing it. But we [broadcasters] handle the length of a piece better. We learn to get to the essence of an issue. We leave out all the adjectives."

He and his colleagues on the broadcast side say they are constantly keeping track of how long the piece is.

"A minute, a minute-thirty," Stokes said, is the most they can do. "The good side of this is you don't have a little gray area, so you don't put in the extra sentence."

Broadcast editorialists may leave out extra words, but they require a lot of other extra elements that make tight demands on time.

"I work with a director who is assigned to me," Neil Heinen said. He also needs "a camera person, prompter, audio" among others. That's just for the studio at WISC-TV, in Madison, Wisconsin. If Heinen wants to tape in the field, which brings immediacy and impact, he needs a "visually relevant spot" and he has to find a photographer, which is not always easy.

By the time you get the "writer part in tune with the speaker part of you," said Peter Kohler of Cablevision, "then

Chapter 9
Time Management

you try for footage—very time-con-suming—dig out tape and work with an editor to roll it in, or you go on-site with a photographer and editor. After that, there's still a lot of work. It's like building a cuckoo clock because you have to come back to the studio and stitch it all together. How do you manage time? You do it right now."

To illustrate, he did the interview for this chapter right on the spot. It didn't take much longer than trying to work out another mutually acceptable time.

That's a good idea for managing your time: Do it now.

From his office on Long Island, east of New York City, Kohler runs a large editorial staff scattered around the metropolitan area.

"We don't all work in one room," he said, "and one can't manage all the time for others." They meet through a weekly conference call and stay in touch by e-mail and individually by phone. "Whoever invented the cell phone was very helpful," he adds.

Most broadcast editorial staffs are small, Stokes pointed out, so the editorial director needs to work efficiently.

"Generally I use the morning to skim the papers and read articles I really need to read," he said. "Then I do the phone calling, then start working on the editorial piece." He has to prepare his weekend program and tape it, and fit in time for public appearances before local groups.

"It used to be that weekends were a great time for sitting around the house and reading for edits coming up," Stokes said, "so Monday I've got a good feel for what I'm going to do. It makes the week more organized."

But even with good planning and organization, he said, "you get one of those weeks where everything's sort of breaking. Then you just scramble. I do a lot of praying and scrambling."

A Time-Management Checklist

1. Use exercise time to work out an idea. Walking or running, or working out on the treadmill or stair-climber, provides a rhythm that lets you concentrate on the lead for a column, the angle for the Sunday editorial, the way to handle a staff member who's proving difficult.

2. Use commuting time to give your mind a break. Letting it rest a bit on the mechanics of driving or the rhythm of the train or bus frees it to be able to take up the hard work of thinking again.

3. Use your daily down time to take a real break from the desk, keyboard and phone. Go out of the office for coffee at a public place, or walk outdoors, or zone out alone in a quiet place for ten minutes.

4. Use the VCR to "control" time. When you tape a program, you can watch it at the time most convenient for you—and you can zip through the commercials and promos to shorten your viewing time.

5. Use the computer to the max: set

Time Management

schedules, respond to e-mail letters, set up a common file for topics the staff will deal with, do research, keep in touch with NCEW colleagues who may be working on similar topics.

TIME MANAGEMENT

Chapter 10

The Future of Editorial Pages

By Lynnell J. Burkett

Will newspapers survive in the twenty-first century?

This book so far has been based on the assumption that the answer is *yes*. It has considered ways for those who work on editorial pages as we know them to do what they always have done, only better.

But some people believe that newspapers will survive only if they change radically, and they question whether the industry is ready to undertake such extensive change.

Even more conservative thinkers, those unwilling to accept that the future of the industry is at stake, likely will concede that the health of newspapers—and of editorial pages—depends on a number of factors. They include:

• Understanding the significance of new media.

• Knowing our audience.

• Having a sure grasp on what we do well.

• Adapting to rapidly changing technology.

• Doing what we do now, but better.

About the author

Lynnell J. Burkett

Lynnell Burkett, editorial page editor of the *San Antonio Express-News,* taught journalism for 15 years at San Antonio College before joining the *San Antonio Light* in 1987. She moved to the *San Antonio Express-News* in 1993 when the *Light* was turned out. While an editor-in-residence at North-western University's Media Management Center in 1998, she wrote *Future Voice— Editorial Pages: Newspapers' Overlooked Strategic Tool.* A member of the executive committee of NCEW, she will become the organization's president in 2004.

Chapter 10
The Future of Editorial Pages

Our survival is at stake

Jon Katz takes the darker view of newspapers' future. He thinks that by refusing to reflect new realities, the leaders of newspapers are committing professional suicide. He takes no pleasure in that opinion, having worked for a number of newspapers, including *The Washington Post, The Boston Globe, The Philadelphia Inquirer* and *Dallas Times Herald,* before moving to television, magazines and, finally, the Internet as a columnist writing about new media. He thinks newspapers must change radically or die.

"Cautious, conservative, constipated"—that's how he described them. As the Internet has provided more people an opportunity to say what they wish, newspapers, he thinks, "have become more conservative, more restrained, not free and, thus, less interesting."

They have had trouble coming to terms with the Internet, he says.

Likewise, he believes the medium has become disconnected from people. Many of his specific criticisms have great implications for editorial pages. Also a First Amendment Center scholar, Katz has outlined his concerns in columns on The Freedom Forum Web site (www.freedom forum.org):

• Graphics: "In recent years, newspapers remain graphically impaired. They have reluctantly turned to color photographs, but seem oblivious to the graphic revolution that has swept magazines and is spreading throughout the World Wide Web."

• Opinion: "As the Net and Web spawn ferocious and idiosyncratic commentary, democratizing opinion all over the country, newspapers cling to stuffy and elitist op-ed pages, where opinion is generally confined to a 'left' and 'right' and voice usually given to elite claques of pundits, academics, authors and CEOs."

• Technology: "Technology, perhaps the central social issue of our times, is spawning a host of stunningly significant stories of great relevance to almost everyone—genetics; artificial intelligence; open-source and free-software movements; patent, copyright and intellectual content questions; super-computing, the explosive rise of the Net, the Web, and e-commerce. . . . The big story in cyberspace isn't the dot-coms thundering onto the Web, but the revolutionary social consequences of a technology that is transforming almost every major social, cultural and political institution in the world, from music to movies to media to commerce and soon, politics and education. You'd think newspapers would have a feast covering great stuff like this, but it's hard to find a newspaper that covers these issues at all, let alone thoroughly."

• Alienation from young readers: "When it comes to the young, the press has reaped precisely what is has sown. Years of hostility to youth culture, inept and short-sighted coverage of technology, and archaic ideas about news and public policy have driven younger consumers away."

By alienating young readers, Katz thinks newspapers are needlessly throwing away their future.

"There's a huge spot for newspapers," he said. "Young people are very eager for papers to be better, but few papers have experimented radically."

Recent research bears out Katz's view on the alienation of young readers. A survey of eighteen- to twenty-four-year-olds by the Round Table Group, a Chicago-based consulting firm of university professors, in the spring of 2000 concluded that the Internet is replacing newspapers and television more rapidly than many observers expected. Of more than one thousand households surveyed, sixty-seven percent of Americans aged eighteen to twenty-four live in households that use the Internet to find key information.

Fifty-nine percent of these young adults report that their households receive more useful information from the Internet than from newspapers, and sixty-eight percent of households with people in this age group say they would more likely consult the Internet to answer a specific question than turn to a newspaper.

These young people are the tail end of Generation X, children of the early Baby Boomers and—of even more concern—the beginning of Generation Y, children of the later Baby Boomers and the first generation that has grown up with the Internet.

Drawing young readers

In his 1997 book, *Growing Up Digital,* author Don Tapscott christened this younger group "The Net Generation," arguing that it is a much more accurate description than Generation Y. Not surprisingly, there are lots of these young people. Tapscott estimated that there would be eighty-eight million youngsters

between the ages of two and twenty-two by the turn of the century. They likely will determine whether newspapers have a future.

What do we know about the Net Generation? Born after 1980, these young people know more than their elders about technology and have no fear of using it.

Although the majority of them have access to the Internet and know how to use it, reading remains important to them. After all, this is the Harry Potter generation, arriving, parents in tow, for the midnight release of the latest J.K. Rowling book.

As Melinda Beck of *The Wall Street Journal* reported in 1997, "At least this generation is reading and being read to. Publishers have responded with an outpouring of titles and series for young readers; annual sales of juvenile books have more than doubled, to $1.4 billion since 1987."

Both traditional and Net marketers have taken note of this trend. As Beck reported, "Companies that sell toys, videos, software and clothing to kids have boomed in recent years. Nine of the ten best-selling videos of all time are animated films from Walt Disney Co. Club Med, the French vacation company, now earns half its U.S. revenues from resorts that cater to families."

Are newspapers spending time preparing for this major generational shift? Are editorial pages noting demographic trends? How will editorial pages draw youngsters, in hopes that they will become adult newspaper readers? Tapscott's method of learning about the Net Generation may offer one clue. He set up an Internet forum

Chapter 10
The Future of Editorial Pages

of three-hundred youngsters aged four to twenty. Tapscott e-mailed his Internet group over a year's time, seeking input for what became his book. Editorial pages that hope to "hook" the younger generation might likewise make special attempts to draw them into discussions and debates over current issues, from politics to pop culture.

What we do well

With the introduction of each new medium, other media have had to reposition themselves, building on their traditional strengths while the new medium brought new vigor to the mix. Most people, even within the newspaper industry, will concede that newspapers no longer hold the edge in breaking news.

Radio, television and the Internet provide almost instantaneous information, often breaking news hours before newspapers are able to. But these other media fall short in a number of areas where newspapers shine— including editorial pages and opinion sections. These pages are crucial to maintaining a number of newspaper strengths. Consider these critical areas:

• Providing credibility.

• Offering context and placing events in perspective.

• Allowing reader participation.

• Connecting with the community.

In a world with an information glut, and where much of the information is either misleading or patently false, newspapers, with their history of providing accurate information, offer credibility. Opinion sections share the reputation for accuracy and fairness that newspapers have built.

Editorial pages provide the soul of the newspaper in providing context and perspective, allowing reader participation and connecting with the community. As leaders of opinion sections seek new ways to become relevant, they never must forget their bedrock strengths.

Adapting to changing technology

As soon as it became clear that the Internet was here to stay, newspapers jumped in, to protect their brands and offer their products online. Although few have devised or discovered a business model that makes providing news, entertainment and opinion on the Web profitable, most people believe it is only a matter of time until that becomes more common.

Meanwhile, newspapers have plunged into the new medium, spending huge resources so that when the break occurs, they can survive.

Michael Zuzel, an editorial writer for *The Columbian* in Vancouver, Washington, sees the venture of putting editorial page content onto the Web as self-defense:

"I'm not so much interested in drawing people to the paper [through the Web site]. I'm more interested in covering our bases. We don't know where electronic is headed. In creating a Web strategy, my interest is principally in covering that base."

He points out that expectations of technology may change tomorrow.

"Who knows? The Internet may seem quaint and obsolete in ten years. But if we constantly expose ourselves to new media, we have a fighting chance when the next medi-

The Future of Editorial Pages

um comes."

The first step for most papers, including their editorial pages, has been to transfer what has appeared on their printed pages onto their Internet sites. Thus, readers are able to go to a Web site and find editorials, columns, cartoons and letters to the editor.

Step two, for many, is to allow readers to hit a button and respond to whatever they are reading, making the entire area *interactive*. This interactivity is a key asset of the new medium.

Another common technique is to link editorial page material to other sites with additional material on the same or related topics. Thus, someone reading an editorial who wants to see the original research material from which the opinion was drawn, or to read more background, can do so with a flick of the wrist.

From there, papers expand in a number of directions. Here are some examples:

• Chat rooms: From any element on the page, readers can move to a discussion site and join others interested in the same topic. A number of newspapers have found this less than helpful because the site is not monitored and, too often, rules governing everything from civility to libel are ignored. Thus, some papers, including my own *San Antonio Express-News,* have chosen to close their chat rooms.

• Forums: Monitored forums are a more successful alternative to chat rooms. These are monitored so the rules can be enforced. An added value can be participation by the writer, whether an editorial writer or a columnist.

• Expanded letters: With unlimited space on the Web, editors can run additional letters to the editor and longer letters than can appear on the printed page.

Arizona

One editorial page editor who is experiencing measurable success on her newspaper's Internet site is Keven Ann Willey of *The Arizona Republic.*

As a former political reporter, she particularly has been interested in the Web page's ability to influence people's relationship to the political process.

First, she noted, is the importance of connecting with those running the newspaper's Web operation.

"I've worked really hard to build the relationship between the editorial page and online," she said. "That's really important. Don't give up. Build relationships at the top level and at the bottom level."

Second, she points out the necessity of thinking carefully about what you wish to accomplish. She suggested "sitting down and removing yourself from the day-to-day routine and capturing the best of what you do."

Although *The Arizona Republic* has undertaken some creative projects, Willey underscored an important point about the directions the page chose: "They evolved organically. They were extended from what we did on the page."

The first example is the newspaper's Scorecard project. Willey said staff members developed a large chart in their boardroom, listing a couple of dozen of the issues most

Chapter 10
The Future of Editorial Pages

important to them. They included specific bills in the legislature on issues they were following. Then they listed the governor and all ninety Arizona legislators, noting for each a happy face or green alien face to depict their position of each of the important issues and bills.

The concept worked so well that eventually they decided it should be available to readers. Besides running it on the pages of an expanded opinion section, they made it available online. Now, in the opinion section of the *Republic's* site, readers will find a searchable Scorecard.

The editorial board explained its purpose for the Scorecard to the site's readers: "Our goal in developing this legislative Scorecard is to help us—and you, the readers—determine which lawmakers are positive forces at the Capitol and which ones are the troublemakers."

Board members explained that they followed what the board identified as key issues, rating the governor and legislators only on issues about which the newspaper had editorialized. The searchable topics include areas such as alcohol abuse, health, kids, tobacco settlements, education, redistricting, general conduct—even miscellaneous. Then, each issue includes a variety of specific topics.

The reader keys in the specific legislator and topic and gets the editorial board's reading on how that legislator is performing, including how the person voted on specific bills.

A second project has been an online questionnaire about key issues from candidates seeking political office in 2000, an undertaking that

Willey describes as extremely labor-intensive. The department sent questionnaires to two hundred seventy-nine Arizona legislative and congressional candidates, surveying them on their stands about a variety of issues facing the state. Then the newspaper posted results online. The first step, of course, was to determine which issues were most important and how to ask key questions, Willey explained.

The candidates could receive a log-on and password and answer the questionnaire electronically, or they could fill out the form and return it to be posted online.

Nearly sixty percent of candidates returned the questionnaires, and Willey said most of the non-responders were candidates without opposition.

Ninety-nine questionnaires were returned electronically, and sixty-seven came manually, requiring that they be keyed into the computer terminal.

In the future, candidates will be required to respond electronically.

Beyond those two major projects, the *Republic's* opinion pages have offered a number of other features on the Web site, in addition to editorials, letters and columns that have run in the newspaper. They include:

• A message board, where readers can respond to a question that is run online each week. For example, the question late in August 2000 was, "How will history remember President Clinton's presidency?"

• A page summarizing election recommendations made during the year 2000. At the end of each editorial is a link to the Web site of the candi-

The Future of Editorial Pages

date the editorial board has endorsed.

• A page on Growth in Arizona, the newspaper's top priority for the year 2000. This brings together everything that has been written on the editorial pages on the topic during the year— editorials, commentaries, reader responses, editorial cartoons.

•Another page that focuses on redistricting, which is referred to as an Area of Emphasis selected by the editorial board for the year. This, again, brings together editorials written during the year that focus on the topic.

How have online readers responded? According to data measured by the newspaper's online department, the opinion pages average forty-eight thousand page views per week, a higher number than the sports department.

From the time the Scorecard was posted on May 1, 2000, until August 14, the Scorecard had received 1,348 page views. From the posting of candidate questionnaires on July 21 until August 13, it received 2,590 page views. In addition, page views of the newspaper's recommendations for voters numbered 14,869 from July 14 to August 13. (The Arizona primary election was September 12.)

Willey sees this as a highly useful part of her department's work. "We think it is of great value. It's a way to get more information directly to the readers."

West Virginia

One person who has had little trouble establishing a good relationship with his newspaper's online operation is Dan Radmacher of *The Charleston Gazette* in West Virginia. That's because, in addition to his duties as editorial page editor of the newspaper, he also became, as he described himself in a 1998 *Masthead* article, "an accidental Webmaster." He went to a meeting at the newspaper to talk about creating a Web site, submitted a few ideas and found himself in charge.

He sees the Internet as a way to expand the reach of newspaper.

"If people are using the Internet to get news and opinion, if we're not there, they'll get it elsewhere."

The Charleston paper has created forums to allow readers to interact. Radmacher refers to it as "online talk radio." He found that the posters are more conservative than the newspaper's print readership, a characteristic they share with talk radio participants. Those who see the newspaper as biased see this as a source of unfiltered opinion.

Radmacher monitors sites, deleting or editing libelous postings. He said he sometimes gets involved and answers questions.

He links to other sites in areas about which the newspaper has done in-depth projects. He also mentions the ease of sending letters to the editor and the possibilities online chat rooms offer for allowing people to talk to reporters, editors and columnists online. "It's important to use tools the Web makes available for reader interaction and do it in a way that doesn't devalue opinion," he said.

Radmacher no longer is running both the editorial page and online service. The newspaper eventually

The Future of Editorial Pages

hired help for the online operation. "We keep talking about ways to expand it, but haven't done it yet."

The Wall Street Journal

One ambitious innovation in online opinion is OpinionJournal .com, a separate Web site from *The Wall Street Journal's* editorial page. While the *Journal* remains the only newspaper that requires readers to pay to access its Web site, its OpinionJournal.com is free. Within its description of itself is the explanation, "Our opinion journalism has from the outset been included in our electronic mother ship, WSJ.com, and we certainly hope that the free sampling in OpinionJournal will attract the attention of a new audience and persuade many of them to become regular subscribers. But we also want to participate more vigorously in and learn more about a new and growing form of communication. . . ."

Easily at hand are the newspaper's editorials, columns and featured article of the day. The site also lists what the *Journal's* opinion page considers favorite Web sites and links to best articles from various sources. There's also a campaign log, and, indeed, the reader of OpinionJournal.com finds many paths that wander directly to wsj.com, with enticements to register for two free weeks' subscription to the full online newspaper. While it may be too early to measure success of this enterprise, the site is attractive and easily navigable. Whether a local editorial page has the resources to undertake such a project and whether it would draw enough viewership would require experimentation to learn.

WISC-TV

Among the few television stations with a full-time editorial director is WISC-TV, Madison, Wisconsin's CBS affiliate and top-rated station. Neil Heinen, the editorial director, hopes to do with his site what he has not been able to do on air—develop an op-ed function, allowing a variety of voices in the community to have their say. Eventually, he would like to see his editorials followed on the site by two or three other views on the same topic.

Right now, he posts his editorials on the site as soon as they are ready, meaning that people often can read them on the station's Web site before they hear them delivered on air. Someday, Heinen points out, those who visit the Web site will be able to hear editorials that have been videotaped. Heinen's station, like owners of other Web sites, continues to redesign the site so that it will be more reader-friendly and make it easier for viewers to respond to what they've read.

His station has been noted for its close cooperation on a variety of projects with the *Wisconsin State Journal*, one of Madison's two newspapers. But the cooperation does not extend to the Web site because that is viewed as competitive.

"We've not figured out how to get over the competitive hurdle there," Heinen explains. But both newspaper and television Web sites link to joint project sites, most notably "We the People," a long-standing voter project on which the two have been partners.

Chapter 10
The Future of Editorial Pages

Convergence

The word "convergence" has gained currency in the media world. Companies are seeking ways to create partnerships involving different media "platforms"—such as newspaper, television and Web site—to jointly use resources in ways that play to the strengths of each. Some newsrooms, with Tribune Media Company newspapers in the forefront, have created joint assignments desks for their newspaper, broadcast and Web operations. Such efforts only will increase.

The *San Antonio Express-News,* with KENS-TV, the local CBS affiliate and top-rated station in the market, has created a new company to run a Web site called MySanAntonio.com, which utilizes material from both newspaper and television.

With the use of joint resources, an *Express-News* editorial board meeting determining whether to endorse a light-rail project for the city became a live Webcast, open to anyone who accessed the Web site. Dubbed a "cybercast," the event featured proponents and opponents of light rail, with questions from the newspaper's editorial board members and reporters. A KENS-TV camera occupied a seat at the table, providing MySanAntonio.com viewers a live view of the proceedings. The results were posted on the Web site; those unable to observe the event live could call it up later on their computers. Views were a bit blurred, and the sound a bit unsynchronized with the video. But these problems will be solved by broadband technology. The newspaper views this as only a beginning. An obvious enhancement will be allowing viewers to participate by sending e-mail questions to participants in the meeting. The possibilities for such activities are as varied as the imagination of the newspaper's editorial page staff.

Three conclusions can be made about the role of editorial page leaders as they incorporate new media into their responsibilities:

• The name of the game is experimentation. Beyond the obvious goal of transferring what appears in print to what is on the Web site, the field is wide open for imagination and creativity.

• *Interactivity* is a key advantage to the Internet. As editorial page people determine what they want to do to enhance their Web presence, they should ask how they enable their audience to communicate with them and with each other.

• No one knows where this grand new experiment is leading. It is unclear whether in ten years working with the Web will be a major part of an editorial page editor's job or whether that idea will have become passe. Furthermore, everything in the world of technology is changing so rapidly that no one is in a position to hazard more than a reasonable guess about this. Looking at next year is looking a long way out.

The September 2000 issue of *American Journalism Review,* in its cover article, "Surviving in Cyberspace," talked about the buckling of the Internet "content" business. It reported that "somewhere between 2,000 and 3,500 dot-com workers lost their jobs delivering news, entertainment and information in May [2000] alone."

The Future of Editorial Pages

The euphoria is gone, the magazine reported, and the understanding has settled in that journalistic success on the Internet is a long-term proposition requiring large expenditures.

Even though working in the Internet world will be a long-term, costly proposition, it is a must. At the same time, those involved with editorial pages must not lose sight of what they do well.

Whatever the "platform," whether in the pages of a daily newspaper, on an Internet Web site or on a television screen, those who work on editorial pages will remain the best source for credible opinions, produced by those with no outside agenda, beholden to no one beyond the newspaper. They will help set the values of the community, reflect those values and, at their best, draw the community together to work on common problems.

As they move into the twenty-first century, editorial page editors and writers will face many challenges—attracting new audiences, dealing with new subjects (from globalization to popular culture), incorporating new media. But their fundamental values and primary tasks will remain the same: a dedication to seeking truth, sharing ideas and shaping the goals and aspirations of their communities and the nation. The need for such a calling will not disappear.

Get Beyond Wood Pulp and Ink
By Michael Zuzel

The editorial page is the original interactive mass medium, but technology offers some opportunities that we'll never have as long as we're married to wood pulp and ink. Here are examples:

• True give and take. An online forum, such as *The Columbian's,* at www.columbian.com/currents, allows readers to engage one another in a true discussion, challenging one another's arguments and defending their own. This can happen on a letters page, but only very slowly, with days or weeks separating call and response, and only if the editor allows the debate to continue instead of cutting it off after the second or third rejoinder, which many of us do. Only when our letters column comes equipped with a "refresh" button will we be able to match the Web browser in this regard. Incidentally, we don't allow anonymous posts in our forum.

• Actual engagement with the messenger. Think of the poor reader who comes upon a rousing debate in the letters column about an article published the previous week, an article that has long since been carted away by the recycling truck. The Web allows debates to be attached directly to the articles in question. The geographical proximity offers more encouragement for people to participate as well as, again, more immediate give and take. For a superb example, check out virtually any article on www.intellectualcapital.com.

• Unlimited news hole. On the Web, there's no line limit. For all those readers who have been told their letters did not run because of lack of space, this alone represents a major breakthrough. *The Oregonian* runs a dozen or so local op-ed pieces every week on its Web site (www.oregonlive.com) that don't appear in print.

• Hyperlinks. Oh, the number of times I've seen a URL on a printed page and unconsciously reached for my mouse to follow the link. On the Web, a reader can cite all manner of documents and authorities, without the need to quote them at length, simply by linking to those sources. Again, this is possible on the printed page. But how many readers really go to the trouble of looking up a Supreme Court case when it's listed by title and year in the newspaper? A hyperlink makes that easy.

About the author
Michael Zuzel

Michael Zuzel is an editorial writer for *The Columbian* in Vancouver, Washington.

Link Opinion Pages to the Internet
By Danny Glover

These helpful tips will connect opinion pages to the Net:

1. Make e-mail addresses mandatory on all columns—and display them prominently, in print and online. Make them part of the byline, which should be as much about accountability to the readers as ego gratification of the writers. Do the same for all editorial board members, if not on the editorials, then in a prominent location/box on the page.

2. Create some kind of "Readers' Log." People like Jim Romenesko, who has a media column at www.poynter.org/medianews/, use Web logs to point people to interesting sites, to critique the sites or to offer brief commentary. They are one of the most popular features of the Internet content world these days. Newspaper readers and the journalists themselves often can benefit from what readers have to say. The cranks may need to be filtered, but that's just the nature of the interactive beast.

Newspapers must accept it. Read more about Web logs at www .content-exchange.com/cx/html/ newsletter/1-25/ws1-25.htm.

The Future of Editorial Pages

3. Start an Interactive Editorial Board. Members of editorial boards talk a lot about community participation in editorial boards, and technology can and should be used to welcome more people into the process. Use a chat format where the board talks about the subjects on the agenda, then welcomes comments from online eavesdroppers. People would never have to leave their homes to participate—and they might even be able to join in the "fun" during breaks at work.

4. Try moderated discussions. Pick one editorial or column a day or a week (maybe on Sundays) and guide the discussion. It will take staff to do that, but readers will appreciate investment in staff time.

About the author

Danny Glover

Danny Glover is managing editor of *National Journal's* Technology Daily.

APPENDIX A

Handy Form Letters

Here are examples of letters that editorial pages send out for a variety of different reasons. They can be used as the basis for responding to readers on issues of common concern, and can be sent by e-mail:

• The "oops, we blew it," letter:

Dear _____,

Nobody is more disturbed by grammatical and other errors in our newspaper than I am. Although it is embarrassing to be called on them, I am gratified to know that avid readers who don't let them slip by still exist.

You ask how this can happen, and my only response is that we are imperfect human beings. Every day we publish the equivalent of a small book and do it on deadline. While we strive to do it cleanly, our intentions are sometimes better than our performance.

Hearing from readers like you is both motivating and instructive. Don't hesitate to write again when we fall short of your expectations.

Sincerely,

• The "try again next time," letter:

Dear _____,

Thank you for sending me your letter to the editor.

You may be aware that we do not have the room to use all of the letters we receive. Unfortunately, we could not use yours this time around.

Thank you for your interest in [newspaper name] and please try us again. Keep in mind that the shorter your letter, the better your chances of being published. We ask that letters be kept under xxx words.

Sincerely,

Appendix A
Handy Form Letters

• The "spare us your poetry," letter:

Dear _____,

Thank you for your submission.

You may not realize that [newspaper name] does not publish poetry. Editors have found from years of experience that publishing even one poem encourages people to send in reams of bad verse—poems that exhibit far less insight and sensitivity than yours and, if published, would crowd out letters on issues of public concern.

Should you feel the need to write a letter to the editor in the form of prose, we'll be happy to consider publishing it.

Sincerely,

• The "not another thank-you note" letter:

Dear _____,

Thank you for your letter.

Because our space is limited, we print only letters that address issues of general public concern. For this reason, [newspaper name] has made it a policy not to publish thank-you notes.

However, I have taken the liberty of passing on your letter to the organization which your letter praises. No doubt those who run [the organization] will appreciate the sentiments you express so sincerely.

Best wishes,

• The "thanks for the column/cartoon, but . . ." letter:

Dear _____,

Thanks for asking if we would be interested in publishing your columns/cartoons.

Although we are not presently looking for a columnist/cartoonist, I appreciate your interest in [newspaper name] and the opportunity to review your work.

My best wishes for a successful career.

Sincerely,

Appendix A
Handy Form Letters

• The "getting to know you" letter to candidates for public office:

Dear _____,

Congratulations on your primary victory.

As is customary, [newspaper name] will be endorsing candidates for the general election. We would welcome an opportunity to learn more about you.

If you are interested in discussing your candidacy, please call me at xxx-xxxx for an appointment. Please call as soon as possible, and in no case later than xxxxxxx. Interviews begin immediately and will be completed by xxxxx.

Whether or not you have the time to come in, we would welcome any background information you want to send us about yourself and your position on issues. I've enclosed a simple résumé form should you wish to use it, as well as a questionnaire about some key issues. Please return both to me in advance of our meeting. My mailing address/e-mail address is xxxxxxxxxxxxxx.

As the election draws nearer, you may receive a similar inquiry from our news department. The information it seeks will be for use in our election guide. While we regret asking you to duplicate your efforts, it is necessary because of different deadlines and different needs. Please respond to the news department as well.

Best wishes for an enlightening campaign.

Sincerely,

• Forms sent to candidates typically ask for the following information:

Name:

Address:

Birthdate and year:

Office sought:

Party affiliation:

Offices previously held:

Occupation:

Education:

Community activities:

Please name the top three issues in the campaign:

APPENDIX B

Cartoons—Staff and Local

By Ronald D. Clark

Why cartoons? Because they're one of the quickest and most successful ways of bringing eyeballs to the opinion pages. Because, as Sue Dewar, cartoonist for the *Ottawa Sun,* says, "A strong cartoon is part of the personality of a newspaper. Because a cartoon can bring readers to the page who are attracted by visual opinions more than words."

Nevertheless, fewer and fewer newspapers employ their own cartoonists. The fifteen hundred or so daily newspapers in the country employed only about one hundred twenty cartoonists, according to a 1995 study by researchers Chris Lamb and Nancy Brendlinger. That number has been steadily declining. To save money, newspapers have increasingly looked to syndicated, rather than staff, cartoonists to parry and jab.

While syndicated cartoonists can engage readers on national and international topics, by definition they have nothing to say about local topics. That's an acceptable tradeoff for some publishers and editorial page editors, who are loathe to stir up controversy that might prompt advertisers or readers to drop the newspaper. But for others, the lack of a local cartoonist is the newspaper equivalent of the local retailer failing to stock an item in heavy demand by customers.

For example, *The Seattle Times,* which has gone without a staff car-

toonist for several years, learned in a reader survey in 1999 that readers want the newspaper to fill that void, said Mindy Cameron, editorial page editor.

If you have the chance to hire a local cartoonist or add a syndicated one, here are some questions you should ask yourself:

• Will the cartoonist express the views of the newspaper or his own, even if they disagree with editorial policy? Newspapers do it both ways, but you should be very clear about your expectations.

• For a local cartoonist, are you looking for someone with additional skills as an illustrator, caricaturist or graphic designer, or someone you expect to only do cartoons?

• How important is it to you that your ideal local cartoonist be able to work in color, do computer-assisted drawings or be able to animate cartoons on your Internet site?

• Do you want a local cartoonist who will draw every day, or do you want to mix local cartoons with syndicated cartoons?

• Do you want your local cartoonist to focus largely on local subjects? Do you want to hire a local cartoonist who has aspirations to be syndicated, even if it means the cartoonist may want to draw more national and international topics than you would prefer in order to meet syndicate requirements?

Cartoons—Staff and Local

Guest cartoons

Since there are many more would-be political cartoonists than openings for them, consider occasionally asking your readers to draw and submit cartoons. You might be surprised at the response.

One surprised editor was Ron Cunningham of *The Gainesville Sun*. He first issued an invitation in the early 1990s. "At the outset, I wasn't expecting much," he said. "While the response couldn't be described as overwhelming, I was pleased and surprised at both the number of submissions and the generally good quality of the work. Ultimately, about forty people responded with cartoons, and most of those were fair to good in both the quality of the art work and the sophistication of the humor." When an opening later occurred for an editorial cartoonist, the *Sun* hired one of those reader-cartoonists.

We at the *Pioneer Press* have been doing this off and on for years, too, and have found illustrators, graphic designers, artists, school classes, retirees and others—including most recently a correctional officer and a secretary—eager to answer the call. Not only is this a technique for broadening reader participation, but also, said Cunningham, "you might uncover a local talent who will be able to produce good quality political cartoons on a regular basis for a reasonable price." That might be especially appealing for newspapers that want local cartoons but can't afford to hire a full-time or part-time cartoonist.

You might spice up the invitation to readers by creating a separate division for school students or young people, and by offering a book of famous cartoons or a dinner with your own cartoonist (assuming you have one) to the entrant whose work you judge the best.

Separating good from bad

Political cartoonists and syndicate salespeople contend that editorial page editors too often don't know good editorial cartoons from bad, or don't have any idea what they want in a cartoonist. So we asked NCEW members what factors would be most important to them in hiring a new political cartoonist. Here are some of the responses we received:

• Harry Austin, *Chattanooga Times* in Tennessee: A student of politics, history, current affairs; someone with decent art skills, sharp wit and an intriguing way of summarizing core issues.

• Jerry Elsea, *Cedar Rapids Gazette* in Iowa: Be clever and well informed. "Minimalist" drawings are fine as long as the cartoonist puts the idea across instantly. The ability to draw a passable caricature helps.

• Larry Reisman, the *Press Journal* in Vero Beach, Florida: Someone who can come up with ideas, knows the issues and can draw well.

• Gale Hammons, *The Modesto Bee* in California: Someone who generates his own ideas and can work with minimal oversight; is innovative (not a carbon copy of syndicated cartoonists); is unpredictable (neither always conservative nor always liberal).

• Ron Dzwonkowski, *Detroit Free Press*: Awareness of issues, insight, artistic ability. Readers have to be able to quickly grasp the subject matter. Someone with an individual style, who is knowledgeable about history, politics, government and the great cartoonists.

• Mindy Cameron, *The Seattle Times:* Proven talent, journalistic instincts, work ethic, ability/desire to be part of a team and not a Lone Ranger.

Responsibilities of the editor

What is the ideal relationship between an editor and a political cartoonist? What is the responsibility of one to the other, and to readers? While generalizing is fraught with danger, some of the best thinking in the business regarding those questions has come from Ed Williams, editorial page editor of *The Charlotte Observer* in North Carolina. He wrote:

"The cartoonist's job is to be provocative. Mine is to decide what a family newspaper will publish. I treat the cartoonist pretty much as a visual columnist, so the standard I apply is not whether the cartoon reflects our editorial position, but whether it makes a point that the general reader of our pages is likely to understand, and whether it is within the rather generous bounds of taste and accuracy that we apply to cartoons.

"We try to think of ways various readers might find the cartoon offensive, so we don't offend any person or group unintentionally."

What should you, as the editor, do when a cartoon provokes many calls or letters from readers? Williams offers this advice:

1. If you get a lot of complaints about a cartoon you don't regret publishing, don't hesitate to explain yourself in the newspaper.

2. If after hearing the complaints you conclude that you shouldn't have published the cartoon, say so in print. It makes no sense to me to defend a decision you've concluded was wrong. Why not be straight with readers about it?

3. If your gut tells you not to run a cartoon, don't run it. Nothing feels worse than publishing something you thought you shouldn't and regretting it later.

4. If you find yourself killing all your cartoonist's best ideas, maybe you need to (a.) find another cartoonist; (b.) decide whether you really want to have a cartoonist; or (c.) send off for one of those exercise machines that Christie Brinkley advertises in the wee hours on cable TV so you can strengthen your stomach muscles.

APPENDIX C

The World Wide Web

BASIC RESEARCH

The Internet has revolutionized the ability of reporters to get information they need, but much of that depends on a good search engine.

Here are a few suggestions:

Search engines

• **Copernic (www.copernic.com)** is powerful search engine that scans other search engines such as AltaVista to find information. It's free, but to use it you have to download the Copernic program onto your computer. After that, a click on an icon will give you an amazingly detailed search in seconds, arranging the results onto an index that you can store indefinitely or delete as you please.

• **Northern Light (www.northernlight.com)** is helpful for finding news and magazine articles, some for free browsing and some for a small, one-time fee.

• **Google (www.google.com)** is a good search engine for simple searches, using a combination of popularity and relevance to return the answer.

• **Dogpile (www.dogpile.com)** can scan the top choices of up to twenty-five search engines and give you a snapshot of each one.

• **AltaVista (www.altavista.com)** offers one the largest databases of information.

• **Hotbot (www.hotbot.com)** is a search engine useful for more complicated searches.

• **Argos (argos.evansville.edu)** is a peer-reviewed search engine specializing in the classics.

People finders

• **Yahoo!** People search, United States **(people.yahoo.com)**
• **Infospace.com (www.infospace.com/)** United States people search site
• **Bigbook (www.bigbook.com)** A United States and Canada phone book site.
• **The Ultimate White Pages (www.theultimates.com/white)** A people search engine, mostly United States.

Library of Congress

Special Collections, manuscript division
(lcweb.loc.gov/spcoll/cdmanu.html) A guide to manuscripts held by the Library of Congress

Appendix C
The World Wide Web

Experts

• Profnet for reporters (**www.profnet.com/reporters.html**) Gives members of the media access to sources experts on various subjects.

Freedom of Information

• **FOI Handbook page (www.rcfp.org/foiact/index.html)** A do-it-yourself guide to using the federal Freedom of Information Act.

• **Public Citizen's guide to FOI (www.citizen.org/litigation/foic/foic.html)** A clearinghouse of information on FOI from Ralph Nader's group.

• **Federal FOI contacts (www.spj.org/foia/foiresources/fedcontacts/ index.htm)** Society of Professional Journalists list of FOI contacts in the United States federal government.

SOME GOOD WEB SOURCES FOR LONG-TERM PROJECTS

Agriculture research

• **United States Department of Agriculture (www.nal.usda.gov/ttic/ tektran/tektran.html)**

• **USDA Statistics Database (www.usda.gov/nass/)**

• **National Agriculture Library (www.nal.usda.gov/)**

• **Agriculture Network Information Center (www.agnic.org/)**

Business/consumer demographic information

• **American City Business Journal (www.bizjournals.com/journals/ demographics)**

• **Business Research Interests (www.brint.com/interest.html)**

• **EconData.Net: Regional Economic Data (www.econdata.net/)**

• **Company Information (www.edgar-online.com/)**

• **Federal Reserve Banks (www.federalreserve.gov/)**

• **Foundation Center (www.fdncenter.org)** Information about foundations

• **Home Mortgage Disclosure Act (www.ffiec.gov/hmda/)** Sources on fair lending

• **IRS Statistics of Income (www.irs.ustreas.gov/prod/tax_stats/index.html)**

• **Cost of Living Calculator (www.newsengin.com/neFreeTools.nsf/CPIcalc)**

• **Non-profits (www.nonprofits.org/)**

The World Wide Web

- **U.S. Department of Labor Occupational Outlook Handbook (stats.bls.gov/ocohome.htm)**
- **The Right-to-Know Network (www.rtk.net/)** Environment, housing, and sustainable development
- **U.S. Bureau of Labor Statistics (stats.bls.gov/)**
- **U.S. Department of Commerce (www.doc.gov/)**

Demography/Land use planning

- **American Planning Association (www.planning.org)**
- **Census 2000 Home Page (www.census.gov)**
- **Citylink (banzai.neosoft.com/citylink/)**
- **The National Trust for Historic Preservation (www.nationaltrust.org/)**
- **Sprawl Resource Guide (www.plannersweb.com/sprawl/home.html)**
- **The Land Trust Alliance (www.lta.org/)**

Courts/law

- **Lawlinks (resource.lawlinks.com/Content/Legal_Research/Court_Decisions/court_decisions.htm)**
- **National Center for State Courts (www.ncsc.dni.us/COURT/SITES/Courts.htm)**
- **National Freedom of Information Coalition (www.reporters.net/nfoic/web/index.htm)**
- **Legal encyclopedia (www.nolo.com/encyclopedia/index.html)**
- **The Reporters Committee for Freedom of the Press (www.rcfp.org/)**
- **Search Systems (www.pac-info.com/)** Public record databases
- **State laws/legislative info (www.washlaw.edu/)**
- **U.S. Supreme Court decisions (supct.law.cornell.edu/supct/)**

Crime

- **Justice Information Center (ncjrs.aspensys.com/)**
- **Law Enforcement Sites (lawenforcement.miningco.com/careers/lawenforcement/)**
- **National Archive of Criminal Justice Data (www.icpsr.umich.edu/NACJD/)**
- **National Center for Juvenile Justice (www.ncjj.org/)**
- **U.S. Department of Justice Bureau of Justice Statistics (www.ojp.usdoj.gov/bjs/)**

Appendix C
The World Wide Web

- States Encyclopedia (www.50states.com/)
- U.S. Census Bureau American Factfinder (www.census.gov/dads/www/what.html)
- The World Wide Web Virtual Library (www.vlib.org/)

Education
- The American Federation of Teachers (www.aft.org/)
- *Education Week* (www.edweek.org/)
- Education World (www.education-world.com/)
- National Center for Education Statistics (nces.ed.gov/)
- The National School Boards Association (www.nsba.org/)
- U.S. Department of Education (www.ed.gov/)

Environment
- Environmental Protection Agency (www.epa.gov/)
- Environmental Resources on the Internet (www.southampton.liunet.edu/library/environ.htm)
- OSHA Enforcement Inspection Reports (www.osha.gov/oshstats/)
- Society of Environmental Journalists (www.sej.org/)

Local governments
- The National Association of Counties (www.naco.org/counties/counties/state.cfm?state=ny)
- The U.S. Conference of Mayors (www.mayors.org/)

Health/medicine
- American Hospital Directory (www.ahd.com/)
- American Medical Association (www.ama-assn.org/)
- Association of Health Care Journalists (www.ahcj.umn.edu/)
- Centers for Disease Control and Prevention National Center for Health Statistics (www.cdc.gov/nchs/)
- Healthgate (www3.healthgate.com/) Medical databases
- National Library of Medicine catalog (www.nlm.nih.gov/locatorplus/)

Appendix C
The World Wide Web

Politics/elections

- Campaign Finance Information Center (www.campaignfinance.org/)
- Campaign PACs (www.mojones.com/coinop_congress/data_viewer/data_viewer.html)
- Census Bureau Voting and Registration (www.census.gov/population/www/socdemo/voting.html)
- Center for Responsive Politics (www.opensecrets.org/home/index.asp)
- FEC Campaign Contribution Reports (www.fec.gov/)
- Go Vote (www.speakout.com/)
- U.S. House of Representatives (www.house.gov/)
- U.S. Senate (www.senate.gov/)
- The White House (www.whitehouse.gov/)

Transportation

- Fatality Analysis Reporting System (www-fars.nhtsa.dot.gov/)
- Federal Aviation Administration Office of System Safety (nasdac.faa.gov/asp/asy_fids.asp)
- U.S. Bureau of Transportation Statistics (www.bts.gov/)
- U.S. Department of Transportation's Office of Highway Policy Information (www.fhwa.dot.gov/ohim/ohimprod.htm)

U.S. Government

- CAP Web: The Internet guide to Congress (www.capweb.net/)
- Fedstats: Links to federal agencies (www.fedstats.gov/)
- National Archives and Records Administration (www.nara.gov/nara/electronic/)
- Thomas Legislative Info on the Internet (thomas.loc.gov/)
- U.S. Department of Labor OSHA (www.osha.gov/)
- U.S. General Accounting Office (www.gao.gov/)

Welfare/social Issues

- U.S. Department of Health and Human Services (www.acf.dhhs.gov/news/welfare/)

Index

Beyond Argument: A Handbook for Editorial Writers

Index

ABOUT THE EDITORS

Maura Casey is associate editorial page editor for *The Day* of New London, Connecticut. She has won numerous state, regional and national journalism awards, including the Scripps Howard Foundation's Walker Stone Award for editorial writing, the Horace Greeley Award, the New England Press Association's highest award for public service journalism, and the Sigma Delta Chi Foundation's Pulliam Editorial Fellowship. A former member of the board of directors of the National Conference of Editorial Writers, Casey holds a B.A. from Buffalo State College and an M.A. in Journalism and Public Affairs from The American University.

Michael Zuzel is an editorial writer and columnist for *The Columbian* in Vancouver, Washington. He won first place for editorials in the Society of Professional Journalists' Pacific Northwest Excellence in Journalism competition, for newspapers with circulations of 50,000 and above, in 1999 and 2000. He is a former member of the board of directors of the National Conference of Editorial Writers and past editor of NCEW's quarterly journal, *The Masthead.* Zuzel has led discussions about online opinion for NCEW, the American Press Institute and the Pacific Northwest Newspaper Association. He has a B.A. in communication from Boise State University.

ABOUT THE ARTISTS

Jeff Danziger is a syndicated cartoonist with Tribune Media Syndicate and is published in about one hundred newspapers. He began cartooning at the *Rutland Herald* in Vermont, worked as a cartoonist at the *Daily News* in New York and for ten years was the political cartoonist for *The Christian Science Monitor.*

Signe Wilkinson has been the cartoonist for the *Philadelphia Daily News* since 1985 and before that was the cartoonist for *The Mercury News* in San Jose, California. She has learned valuable lessons from each of the four different editorial page editors with whom she has been privileged to work. She won the Pulitzer Prize for Editorial Cartooning in 1992. Other honors include being named "Official State Vegetable Substitute" by the speaker of the Pennsylvania House of Representatives in 1989.

Anders Ramberg, who designed *Beyond Argument,* is design director for the *Star Tribune* in Minneapolis.

About the Foundations

The **Scripps Howard Foundation** is the corporate foundation of The E.W. Scripps Company. Its mission is to advance the cause of a free press through support of excellence in journalism, quality journalism education and professional development. The foundation helps build healthy communities and improve the quality of life through support of sound educational programs, strong families, vital social services, enriching arts and culture and inclusive civic affairs, with a special commitment to the communities in which Scripps does business.

Scripps Howard Foundation
P.O. Box 5380
312 Walnut Street
Cincinnati, Ohio 45201
Phone (513) 977-3035
Fax (513) 977-3800
Web site address: www.scripps.com/foundation

The **NCEW Foundation** is the education arm of the National Conference of Editorial Writers. Its many activities have included sponsorship of the annual Minority Writers Seminar, which exposes experienced minority journalists to the craft of opinion writing; presentation of the annual Barry Bingham Sr. Fellowship to academic leaders for advancing minority students in journalism careers; financial support for college journalism students to participate in critique sessions at NCEW's annual conventions; and underwriting of *The Masthead,* NCEW's quarterly professional journal.

NCEW Foundation
6223 Executive Boulevard
Rockville, Maryland 20852
Phone (301) 984-3015
Fax (301) 231-0026
E-mail: ncewhqs@erols.com
Web site address: www.ncew.org